INCOME AND EMPLOYMENT
IN THE SOUTHEAST

A UNIVERSITY OF
KENTUCKY STUDY

Income and Employment in the Southeast

A STUDY IN CYCLICAL BEHAVIOR

by

L. Randolph McGee

UNIVERSITY OF KENTUCKY PRESS
Lexington, 1967

Copyright © 1967 by the University of Kentucky Press

Library of Congress Catalog Card No.
67-17849

ACKNOWLEDGMENTS

Most of the basic research for this study was finished in the summer of 1963 at Tulane University. For their helpful comments and guidance, I wish to express my appreciation to Professors Seymour S. Goodman and W. David Maxwell. I also wish to express my appreciation to Dr. John L. Fulmer, Director, Bureau of Business Research, University of Kentucky, for his comments concerning the conclusions in Chapter 7. Facilities were provided by the Tulane Computer Center for seasonally adjusting the data. During the summer of 1963 my research was financed in part by a grant from the Inter-University Committee for Economic Research on the South and by a Public Affairs grant from Tulane University. My wife, Dottie, shared most of the burden of typing.

CONTENTS

ACKNOWLEDGMENTS	*page* v
TABLES	ix
1. INTRODUCTION	1
2. INCOME	15
Aggregate Personal Income	16
Per Capita Personal Income	18
Cash Receipts From Farm Marketings	22
Average Weekly Earnings	25
Summary	27
3. AGGREGATE AGRICULTURAL AND NONAGRICULTURAL EMPLOYMENT	28
Agricultural Employment	29
Total Nonagricultural Employment	31
Summary	34
4. COMMODITY-PRODUCING INDUSTRIES EMPLOYMENT	36
Total Commodity-Producing Sector	37
Mining	40

Contract Construction	43
Manufacturing	47
Durable-Goods Manufacturing	51
Nondurable-Goods Manufacturing	54
Average Weekly Hours of Production Workers in Manufacturing	57

5. SERVICES INDUSTRIES EMPLOYMENT	66
Total Services Sector	67
Transportation and Public Utilities	70
Wholesale and Retail Trade	74
Finance	79
Services and Miscellaneous Industries	83
Government	87
Summary	91

6. EFFECT OF INDUSTRY-MIX	94
Nonagricultural Employment	97
Commodity-Producing Employment	99
Services Employment	101
Manufacturing Employment	103
Conclusions	106

7. CONCLUSION	108
Summary of Findings	109
Conclusions	113

APPENDIXES

A. Sources of Data	119
B. Southeast and Non-Southeast	124
INDEX	141

1

INTRODUCTION

𝒯HE STUDY of regional business fluctuations has not received the consideration it deserves, particularly in view of the growing interest in regional economic development. A few writers have demonstrated clearly that cyclical fluctuations differ between regions within the United States.[1] Very

[1] George H. Borts, "Regional Cycles of Manufacturing Employment in the United States, 1914-1953," *Journal of the American Statistical Association*, LV (March 1960), 151-211; (reprinted by National Bureau of Economic Research as Occasional Paper 73, 1960); Gerhard Bry, "Business Cycle Indicators for States and Regions," *Interstate Conference on Labor Statistics*, U. S. Bureau of Labor Statistics, 1961; Gerhard Bry and Charlotte Boschaw, "Nine Business

little, however, has been done with cycles in the South. This study analyzes the behavior of four cycles of income and employment in the Southeastern United States since World War II and compares this behavior with that of income and employment in the nation as a whole.[2] In addition to comparing the Southeast with the United States, it makes a summary comparison between the Southeast and the non-Southeast. With the current emphasis on the economic development of the South, an analysis of the region's business cycles could add much to an understanding of its recent growth.

A long period of time, say more than fifty years, may reveal economic fluctuations of various lengths. The shortest of these fluctuations, disregarding seasonal and random variations, are most commonly referred to as "business cycles." And the most widely accepted definition of "business cycles" is the one used by the National Bureau of Economic Research: "Business cycles are a type of fluctuation found in the aggregate economic activity of nations that organize their work mainly in business enterprise; a cycle consists of expansion occurring at about the same time in many economic

---

Cycle Indicators in Nine States," *Proceedings of 21st Interstate Conference on Labor Statistics*, U. S. Bureau of Labor Statistics, 1963; Frank A. Hanna, "Cyclical and Secular Changes in State Per Capita Income, 1929-50," *Review of Economics and Statistics*, XXXVI (August 1954), 320-30; Philip Neff and Annette Weifenbach, *Business Cycles in Selected Industrial Areas* (Berkeley: University of California Press, 1949); Paul B. Simpson, *Regional Aspects of Business Cycles and Special Studies of the Pacific Northwest*, mimeographed, University of Oregon, 1953; and the following articles by Rutledge Vining: "Location of Industry and Regional Patterns of Business-Cycle Behavior," *Econometrica*, XIV (January 1946), 37-66, "The Region as an Economic Entity and Certain Variations to be Observed in the Study of Systems of Regions," *American Economic Review*, Papers and Proceedings, XXXIX (May 1949), 89-119, and "Regional Variations in Cyclical Fluctuations Viewed as a Frequency Distribution," *Econometrica*, XIII (July 1945), 183-213.

[2] In chronological order these four cycles, measured from trough to trough, are: October 1945–October 1949; October 1949–August 1954; August 1954–April 1958; and April 1958–February 1961. U. S. Bureau of the Census, *Business Cycle Developments*, various issues.

activities, followed by similarly general recessions, contractions, and revivals which merge into the expansion phase of the next cycle; this sequence of changes is recurrent but not periodic; they are not divisible into shorter cycles of similar character with amplitudes approximating their own."[3]

Specific cycles, according to the National Bureau of Economic Research, are "wave-like movements, the duration of which is of the same order as that of business cycles . . . [which are] peculiar to a series."[4] The concept of specific cycles is of primary concern here since the analysis is concerned with particular series rather than with the aggregate economy.

Two points should be noted with respect to the concept of cycles. First, when peaks and troughs are labeled for the aggregate economy, these dates are commonly referred to as "reference cycle" dates; hence, the term "reference cycle" is often used interchangeably with the term "business cycle." And, second, empirical studies of cycles generally consider the entire period of expanding economic activity as the expansion phase and the entire period of declining economic activity as the contraction phase.

Although the few existing empirical studies of regional business cycles leave many interesting questions unanswered, industrial composition is generally thought to be the most influential factor in determining cyclical behavior within a region. The relation between industry-mix and regional cyclical behavior is illustrated best in studies by Rutledge Vining. In a series of articles, Professor Vining demonstrates first the existence of regional business cycles and then investigates the relevance of industrial location to business-cycle analysis.[5] He classifies all industries into two categories: "primary" or "carrier" and "residentiary" or "passive."[6]

[3] A. F. Burns and W. C. Mitchell, *Measuring Business Cycles* (New York: National Bureau of Economic Research, 1946), 3.
[4] *Ibid.*, 24.
[5] See articles by Rutledge Vining cited in footnote 1, above.
[6] Vining, "Location of Industry and Regional Patterns of Business-Cycle Behavior," 40.

Primary industries produce goods which are marketed nationally and residentiary industries produce goods marketed mostly within a region. He believes that the responsiveness of a region to business fluctuations is determined by the character of primary industries; residentiary industries act only passively to cyclical forces. Consequently, the cyclical behavior of residentiary industries within a given region is likely to be more similar to some "primary" industry in that region than to their counterparts in other areas of the nation.[7]

None of the studies of regional cycles or of regional economic growth is thorough enough to encompass the entire regional economy. But most of them analyze, in some form, two of the most important economic indicators: income and employment; and the underlying determinant of their growth and stability is usually attributed to the particular industrial composition of a region. With respect to the comparative growth of regions, recent empirical studies suggest that in the South, despite relative gains in some categories, the rate of growth of income (or its major components) and employment has not kept pace with the nation as a whole.[8] As a result, some writers have dubbed the South a "slow-growth" region, and have attributed this slow growth primarily to an adverse industry-mix.

If the industry-mix of a region influences the rate and direction of economic growth and also determines the cyclical stability of a region, could there be some specific relationship between economic growth and economic stability? Several economists have been interested in this question. Schum-

[7] For an excellent summary of Professor Vining's work see Vining, "The Region as an Economic Entity and Certain Variations to be Observed in the Study of Regions," especially pp. 103-104.

[8] See Frank A. Hanna, *State Income Differentials, 1919-1954* (Durham, N. C.: Duke University Press, 1959); Edgar S. Dunn, Jr., *Recent Southern Economic Development as Revealed by the Changing Structure of Employment* (Gainesville, Fla.: University of Florida Press, 1962); and Harvey S. Perloff and others, *Regions, Resources and Economic Growth* (Baltimore: Johns Hopkins Press, 1960).

peter, Hicks, Duesenberry, Kaldor, and Smithies,[9] to mention a few, have attempted to show on a theoretical basis this relation between growth and cyclical stability; others have expressed implicitly or explicitly this relationship through empirical studies. From the empirical studies one discovers two diametrically opposed hypotheses. One hypothesis suggests that slow-growth regions experience greater cyclical stability than fast-growth regions,[10] while the other suggests the opposite relation between growth and stability.[11] At least one study implies that there is no relation between growth and cyclical stability.[12]

If economic growth is understood as a secular phenomenon, then whether or not the Southeastern United States is a "slow-growth" region can be determined only by examination, analysis, and comparison of economic time series spanning a period of time substantially longer than a decade. Thus, evidence taken from the postwar experience alone

[9] Joseph A. Schumpeter, *Theory of Economic Development* (Cambridge: Harvard University Press, 1934); John R. Hicks, *A Contribution to the Theory of the Trade Cycle* (Oxford: Clarendon Press, 1949); James S. Duesenberry, *Business Cycles and Economic Growth* (New York: McGraw-Hill Book Co., Inc., 1958); N. Kaldor, "The Relation of Economic Growth and Cyclical Fluctuations," *Economic Journal*, LXIV (March 1954); and Arthur Smithies, "Economic Fluctuations and Growth," *Econometrica*, XXV (January 1957).

[10] See R. L. Steiner, "Interregional Variations in Economic Fluctuations—Discussion," *American Economic Review*, Papers and Proceedings, XXXIX (May 1949), 133. This hypothesis appears to be implied by A. F. Burns in "Long Cycles in Residential Construction," *The Frontiers of Economic Knowledge* (New York: National Bureau of Economic Research, 1954). For a specific treatment of the problem, see Borts, 152, 183-85. Borts notes some exceptions but observes that "the continuation of (a) high growth rates and wide fluctuations and (b) low growth rates and mild cycles are found more frequently than their opposites" (p. 152).

[11] See Harry Jerome, *Migration and Business Cycles* (New York: National Bureau of Economic Research, 1926), 244; and Wesley C. Mitchell, *What Happens During Business Cycles* (New York: National Bureau of Economic Research, 1951), 20.

[12] Philip Neff, "Interregional Cyclical Differentials: Causes, Measurement, and Significance," *American Economic Review*, Papers and Proceedings, XXXIX (May 1949), 105-19.

may be insufficient to justify drawing conclusions regarding relative growth. Perhaps all that can really be established with a fair degree of reliability, on the basis of the postwar years alone, is the influence of different industrial compositions on the relative cyclical stability of the Southeast and the United States as a whole as may be revealed by disaggregated series of income and employment. Whether or not there exists some substantial association of cyclical stability with rate and direction of secular change during the postwar period (insofar as a relatively unchanging industry-mix may underlie both movements, though perhaps differing in extent of influence on each) can only be a matter for speculation.

That the Southeast is a slow-growth region, however, has been strongly suggested by previous empirical studies. If we assume that this slow growth has prevailed throughout the postwar period, then what relative cyclical behavior should we expect in the Southeast? Borts' study is certainly the most thorough investigation of the relationship of growth to cyclical stability. He concluded, with some reservations, that there is generally a positive relation between growth and cycle amplitudes. If we accept his findings, then we would expect cycle amplitudes to be smaller in the Southeast than in the nation as a whole.

Professor Borts has also suggested a relation between growth and intracycle amplitudes which is of interest. He found generally that strongly growing states had stronger expansions than weaker growing states and that strongly growing states had weaker contractions than the weaker growing states, noting that the greatest difference was found in the expansions.[13] If the Southeast is a slow-growth region, we would expect smaller expansions and larger contractions for the Southeast than for the nation as a whole.

Although the present study is not an attempt to measure the trend underlying cyclical movements in the Southeast, the analysis of cycles should reveal the nature of short-run increases or decreases in economic time series in the South-

[13] Borts, 160.

east relative to the United States. The implications of the results of this analysis as pertains to industry-mix, growth and cyclical stability are discussed in the final chapter.

Three measures of cyclical fluctuations are used in this study: timing, duration, and cycle amplitudes. These measures of a particular series of data for the Southeast are compared with those of corresponding series for the United States as a whole. From a comparison of timing, it can be determined whether a Southeastern series tended to lead or lag the corresponding national series; a comparison of durations determines whether or not the full cycles, and intracycle phases, tended to be longer or shorter in the Southeast; and comparison of cycle amplitudes is the measure used to indicate the relative severity of cyclical fluctuations in the Southeast. In addition to comparing corresponding series in the Southeast and the nation, the cyclical behavior of a component series in the Southeast is compared with its parent series and with other component series (when appropriate) in the Southeast.

In order that specific cycles of each series might be analyzed within the same general framework, the four postwar cycles are referred to, in the present study, as Cycle I, Cycle II, Cycle III, and Cycle IV. Of course, specific cycle turning points did not always fall within the same year as the turning points of the reference cycle. But for those series which cover the period 1945-1961, Cycle I indicates the first specific cycle of a series since the war, Cycle II indicates the second cycle since the war, etc. The dates of the turning points are also indicated in the table pertaining to a particular series.

The United States totals used in the present study include the forty-eight states and the District of Columbia which form the contiguous United States. The Southeastern region here includes the following states: Alabama, Arkansas, Florida, Georgia, Kentucky, Louisiana, Mississippi, North Carolina, South Carolina, Tennessee, Virginia, and West Virginia. This is the U.S. Department of Commerce classification of the Southeast and is adopted for this analysis because of its frequent use in regional economic studies.

The procedure employed by the National Bureau of Economic Research in analyzing specific cycles, with only slight modification, is used in this analysis.[14]

Dating Specific Cycles

The initial step in determining specific cycle dates is the examination of the raw data to determine the presence of seasonal fluctuations. When a series indicates the influence of seasonal variations, it is adjusted to "eliminate" this influence. All of the data used in this study are seasonally adjusted, with the exception of personal income.[15] Personal income data were seasonally adjusted prior to publication and the original raw data were not available.

The seasonally adjusted and the original data are customarily plotted on semilogarithmic graph paper.[16] The series is then scrutinized carefully for turning points and each peak and trough is labeled. Most of the series used in this study revealed distinct peaks and troughs. But in some series the turning points are not easily ascertained. To cope with these peculiar series a set of rules has been established by the National Bureau.[17] These rules were followed, with some modification, in this analysis. When a series is increasing or decreasing rapidly there may be no absolute change

[14] For a thorough discussion of the National Bureau of Economic Research method, see Burns and Mitchell, Chapters 4 and 5.

[15] The seasonal adjustment method used is the X-8 electronic generator computer method developed by the Bureau of Census. This method is explained in Julius Shiskin, "Electronic Computer Seasonal Adjustments, Test and Revision of U.S. Census Methods," in *Seasonal Adjustment on Electronic Computers*, Proceedings of an International Conference held in Paris, November, 1961, (Paris: Organization for Economic Co-operation and Development, 1961), 70-150.

[16] Most of the series analyzed in the present study revealed cyclical fluctuations more clearly when plotted on regular graph paper. For this reason, semilogarithmic graph paper was used only for those series which did not reveal distinct cycles when plotted on regular graph paper.

[17] Burns and Mitchell, 58-64.

in the direction of the series during the expansion and contraction phases, respectively. In such cases, the cyclical influence is reflected only through changes in the rates of increase or decrease. For example, a decline in the rate of increase of a rapidly increasing series is treated as a contraction phase. Similarly, an increase in the rate of decrease of a rapidly declining series is also treated as a contraction phase. Series of this type, however, create no serious problem if they are relatively smooth. The most serious difficulty arises when a decision must be made between competing peaks or troughs. If a series reveals two or more crests in the vicinity of the initial contraction, the general rule is to average the values around each crest and select from the group with the highest average the month with the highest value as representative of the peak. When competing low points occur, the trough is selected accordingly: the month with the lowest value within the group with the lowest average is selected as the trough. Another problem arises when a series has a flat crest or bottom. The general rule in this case is to select the last month of the plane to represent the respective turning points.[18] These are the general rules which are followed, but no set of rules covers all possible conditions. Needless to say, the selection of turning points involves a certain amount of personal judgment. Consequently, different investigators using the same data may disagree on the selection of exact turning points. However, in all questionable cases the reference-cycle and specific-cycle dates established by the National Bureau of Economic Research were used in the present study as guides in the determination of turning points. Especial caution was taken to ensure consistency in the treatment of a particular series

[18] This rule was not followed under certain circumstances. If a series was rapidly increasing, a "flat crest" indicated a considerable decrease in the rate of change. In such a case, the first month of the plane more properly represented the peak. The last month of a plane at the lower level of fluctuation, however, was more appropriate for the trough. This reasoning was applied to a rapidly declining series, *mutatis mutandis*. These deviations from the NBER procedure were few.

for the Southeast and the corresponding series for the United States as a whole. This, of course, was a necessary precaution since the two series were directly compared with each other.

After each peak and trough is labeled, the series is then marked off into separate cycles. Each cycle is measured from trough to trough, subject to the constraint that no cycle be less than fifteen months or more than twelve years in duration. Most of the series analyzed in this study revealed four complete cycles during the postwar period which corresponded roughly to the four general reference cycles dated by the National Bureau of Economic Research.

Leads and lags are measured by using the national average as a standard. That is to say, the comparison of timing shows the number of months by which a series in the Southeast led or lagged the corresponding series in the United States. Since cycles are measured from trough to trough, the terminal trough of one cycle (other than the final cycle) is the initial trough of the following cycle. This raises the problem of identifying the particular cycle to which a difference in timing at a terminal trough should be attributed. Suppose the Southeast led the nation by three months at the terminal trough of Cycle I. If the comparison is made for the initial and terminal troughs of a cycle, this lead will show up again at the initial trough of Cycle II. This, of course, is redundant. When constructing tables of comparisons, I considered only the peaks and terminal troughs. This means that the initial trough of Cycle I (or the first cycle of the series) is not included in the comparison of leads and lags presented in the tables in the text. But the comparison does include the same number of troughs as there are peaks, which is important when computing and comparing average lead or lag.[19]

[19] There were generally four complete cycles in a series during the postwar period. There were, therefore, four peaks and four terminal troughs. If the initial trough of the first cycle were included in computing the average lead or lag, the average for peaks would include four values while the average for troughs would include five values.

Cycle Relatives

After each series has been divided into separate cycles, an average of all the monthly values within a cycle is computed. A weight of one-half is given each trough value to prevent a downward bias.[20] This monthly average is the "cycle base" upon which cycle relatives are computed. In computing cycle relatives, the initial step is to construct a three-month average centered on each turning point. This average is used to represent the peak and trough values instead of the actual value appearing during the month of the respective turning point.[21] Using this three-month average, each peak and trough is expressed as a percentage of the cycle base. The resulting percentages are the cycle relatives.[22]

Cycle Amplitudes

The expansion amplitude is determined by taking the difference between the cycle relative representing the peak and the cycle relative representing the initial trough; the contraction amplitude is the difference between the cycle relative representing the peak and the cycle relative repre-

[20] Each cycle of a positive series has two troughs and only one peak. Inclusion of the full values of both troughs would, therefore, cause a downward bias. Cycles of inverted series, on the other hand, are measured from peak to peak; consequently, the peaks of these cycles are weighted one-half. There were no inverted series in this study. However, a few series only covered the contraction phase of the initial cycle. For these series, the cycle base for the initial cycle was computed to an inverted basis, i.e., from the peak of the initial cycle to the peak of the following cycle, with a weight of one-half given to each peak.

[21] This eliminates erratic fluctuations immediately around the turning points. An exception is made to the three-month average rule when one of the phases of a cycle is so short that all of the values within this phase would be used when computing the averages of the peak and the trough. Another exception is made for instances in which a peak month is followed by an extremely low value or the trough month is followed by an extremely high value.

[22] This method of computing cycle relatives eliminates the intercycle trend but does not eliminate the intracycle trend. Reasons for not adjusting a series for the trend component are discussed in Burns and Mitchell, 65. A more thorough discussion of the effects of secular trend on cyclical measures is presented in *ibid.*, Chapter 6.

senting the terminal trough. If the cycle relative of the peak is larger than the cycle relative of the initial and terminal troughs (the normal case), the expansion amplitude is preceded by a plus sign and the contraction amplitude by a minus sign, indicating the direction of the fluctuation. The full-cycle amplitude includes the amount of fluctuation in both directions; that is, it is the sum of expansion and contraction often reversing the sign of the latter. In the present study no sign is given to the full-cycle amplitude.[23] By using this method, a cycle which has a minus expansion and a minus contraction would have a full-cycle amplitude which is the difference between the amplitudes of intracycle phases. Similarly, the same would be true if both the expansion and the contraction amplitudes were positive.

Averages

The average lead or lag at peaks or troughs is simply the average of all the leads or lags for the cycles covered. However, average duration and average amplitude need further explanation. Only complete cycles are included in these averages. For example, some series which do not cover the full postwar period include one additional cycle phase—the contraction phase. Therefore, an average of all the values in the several contraction phases should include, in its computation, one item more than in the corresponding averages for the expansion phase and the full cycle. This computation could lead to a serious bias in the comparison of the average contraction to the average expansion. To avoid such a bias, the extra contraction phase is not included in the average duration or average amplitudes. There is no similar problem in averaging leads and lags since the com-

[23] The sign preceding the expansion and contraction amplitudes is a convention which indicates the direction of the cyclical movement. And this is important. But a sign preceding a full-cycle amplitude would be ambiguous, for we can tell nothing about the directions of the cyclical fluctuations without examining the expansion and contraction amplitudes.

putation of a contraction phase necessitates knowledge of the date of the peak as well as the following trough.

Another question arises when amplitudes within a particular column have different signs. To be consistent with the procedure set out in the preceding section, one cannot disregard the signs within a column, in computing the average. Since it is possible to have a negative average expansion amplitude or a positive contraction amplitude, the sign precedes these averages. But it is not necessary to give the average full-cycle amplitude a sign, for the full-cycle amplitude of each cycle has already taken into account the signs of the intracycle phases.

Significant Difference

In interpreting the significance of the number of months by which the Southeast led or lagged the nation, some standard of significant differences in timing had to be established. The standard used in this study was three months.[24] If the Southeast led or lagged the United States at any turning point by less than three months, this difference in timing is considered insignificant. This same standard is applied to differences of duration.

Weights

Each series compared is prefaced by some figures concerning the changes of that series in the Southeast relative to the United States. These computations were made for the purpose of indicating the weights of the series and are not presented as a measure of long-term growth. As noted previously, the period covered is probably too short to measure underlying trends.

[24] This standard is somewhat arbitrary. Since, for purposes of measuring amplitudes, the turning points were represented by a three-month average, a difference of one or two months would be included in the three-month average for the Southeast and the United States. Therefore, a three-month standard seemed consistent with the measures of amplitudes.

Overall differences in timing and amplitudes between corresponding series in the Southeast and the nation as a whole were not substantial except for a few series. And since income and employment do not encompass the entire economic activity of a region, it was not possible to determine concretely whether the Southeast was more or less cyclically sensitive than the United States as a whole. However, the full-cycle amplitudes of the broadest aggregates examined suggest that the Southeast was slightly more sensitive during the postwar period.

Southeastern nonagricultural employment experienced longer periods of expansion and shorter periods of contraction coupled with larger expansion amplitudes and smaller contraction amplitudes than the corresponding segment of the national economy. These differences were only slight in most cases, but they were persistent enough to question the slow-growth label as applied to Southeastern nonagricultural employment.

The industry-mix of Southeastern nonagricultural industries during the postwar period appears to have been more favorable, cyclically, than it would have been if this segment of the Southeastern economy had been made up of the same industry composition as the nation as a whole.

2

INCOME

*I*DEALLY, income should be analyzed by first examining the relative cyclical behavior of Southeastern aggregate income and then its various components. The lack of suitable data for the Southeastern states, however, precludes a good breakdown of income by source.[1] Therefore, this chapter is limited to a comparison of quantitative measures of

[1] Personal income by source of origin is available on a monthly basis for the United States. These figures are found in the August issues of *Survey of Current Business*, published by the U.S. Bureau of Census. However, this breakdown of personal income is not available for states or regions.

cyclical fluctuations for the United States and the Southeast based on four income series. Two of these series, personal income and per capita personal income, are aggregates; and, the other two, cash receipts from farm marketings and average weekly earnings of production workers in manufacturing, are not, strictly speaking, components of the two aggregates. However, the latter two series are related to two important sectors of the economy and should provide some insights into any differential cyclical behavior noted for Southeastern personal income.

Monthly figures for the Southeast are available for personal income and per capita personal income since 1947; these data permit investigation of three complete cycles and the contraction phase of the first cycle. Figures for cash receipts from farm marketings and average weekly earnings of production workers in manufacturing are available only since 1950.

AGGREGATE PERSONAL INCOME

Total personal income in the United States increased from $189.1 billion in 1947 to $412.3 billion in 1961, an average increase of 7.9 percent per year.[2] In 1947 total personal income in the twelve Southeastern states was $28.4 billion and by 1961 it had increased to $65.3 billion, an average annual increase of 8.6 percent. As a percentage of the national total, however, personal income in the Southeast made very little gain over this period, increasing by only 0.8 of one percentage point (from 15.0 percent to 15.8 percent). In 1961 the Southeastern region had 21.7 percent of the total United States population but only 15.8 percent of the nation's total personal income.

[2] Personal income data for the period 1947-1958 are from *Business Week*, Supplement, March 28, 1959, and data for the period since 1958 are from regular issues of *Business Week*. Data are not available on a monthly basis for years prior to 1947. See Appendix A for further description and evaluation of these data.

TABLE 2-1
Turning Points, Durations, and Amplitudes of Cycles in Total Personal Income, United States and Southeast

Cycle	Turning points			S.E. lead (−) or lag (+) (months)		Durations (months)			Amplitudes		
	Init. Trough	Peak	Term. Trough	Peak	Trough	Expan.	Contr.	Full Cycle	Expan.	Contr.	Full Cycle
Cycle I											
U.S.	(a)	9/48	8/49	+1.0	0.0	(a)	11.0	(a)	(a)	−3.7	(a)
S.E.	(a)	10/48	8/49			(a)	10.0	(a)	(a)	−5.9	(a)
Cycle II											
U.S.	8/49	7/53	12/53	0.0	0.0	47.0	5.0	52.0	+33.2	−1.1	34.3
S.E.	8/49	7/53	12/53			47.0	5.0	52.0	+35.1	−1.1	36.2
Cycle III											
U.S.	12/53	8/57	12/57	0.0	0.0	44.0	4.0	48.0	+21.2	−1.3	22.5
S.E.	12/53	8/57	12/57			44.0	4.0	48.0	+23.7	−4.0	27.7
Cycle IV											
U.S.	12/57	7/60	1/61	0.0	0.0	31.0	6.0	37.0	+17.0	−2.1	19.1
S.E.	12/57	7/60	1/61			31.0	6.0	37.0	+19.9	−2.1	22.0
Average[b]											
U.S.				+0.3	0.0	40.7	5.0	45.7	+23.8	−1.5	25.3
S.E.						40.7	5.0	45.7	+26.2	−2.4	28.6

[a] Data not available.   [b] Each column averaged separately.
Source: See Appendix A.

Timing and Durations

The cyclical behavior of aggregate personal income in the Southeast relative to the United States (Table 2-1) shows that timing in Southeastern personal income was virtually synchronous with timing in total personal income for the United States; the only difference was an insignificant lag of 1.0 month by the Southeastern series at the peak of Cycle I.

With this close conformity of timing one would expect very little difference in the duration of cycles and intracycle phases between the two areas. The only difference between durations of any cycle or intracycle phase for the Southeast and the nation occurred during the contraction of Cycle I, when the contraction phase was only 1.0 month shorter for the Southeast than for the United States.

Amplitudes

Although timing of turning points and cyclical durations were similar for the Southeast and the United States, average amplitudes of cyclical fluctuations in Southeastern personal income were larger for the full cycle and both intracycle phases, relative to average amplitudes in national personal income. Comparison of amplitudes for individual cycles shows Southeastern personal income fluctuated more than national personal income during all three expansion periods and the three full cycles. Moreover, contraction amplitudes were larger for the Southeast during two of the four contraction phases, and during the other two periods of contraction the amplitudes were the same for personal income in both areas.

PER CAPITA PERSONAL INCOME

Although per capita personal income is another measure of personal income, it is significant because it shows the influence of population changes.³ Should population in the Southeast change relative to the national total during the intracycle phases, this change could alter the relative cyclical behavior of per capita personal income in the Southeast.⁴

Per capita personal income increased rather steadily in the United States and the Southeast over the period 1947-1961. Per capita personal income in the United States was $1,318 in 1947; by 1961 it had increased to $2,265. This was an overall increase of 71.8 percent and an average annual increase of 4.8 percent—a smaller increase than that of total personal income.

In the Southeast, per capita personal income increased from $886 in 1947 to $1,654 in 1961, representing a total increase of 86.7 percent, or an average annual increase of 5.8 percent. Thus, the rate of increase of per capita personal income was greater in the Southeast than for the nation as a whole. This is further substantiated by the relative share of per capita personal income in the Southeastern states which was 67.2 and 73.0 percent of the national average in 1947 and 1961, respectively. Southeastern per capita personal income is still low relative to the United States, and, although

---

³ Per capita personal income, for the United States and the Southeast, is derived from personal income figures reported in *Business Week* and population figures were derived from the data reported in U.S. Bureau of the Census, *Current Population Reports*, p. 25. See Appendix A for further description and evaluation of these data.

⁴ For example, suppose there is a net out-migration from the Southeast to other areas of the United States during periods of expansion and that there is an opposite net movement during periods of contraction. Further, suppose all migrants to and from the Southeast are from the ranks of the unemployed and remain unemployed after relocating. They would not be contributors to total personal income (except as recipients of transfer payments) in either area, but the relative loss of (low-wage) population in the Southeast during expansion would affect per capita personal income in a positive manner and conversely during periods of contraction. However, all migrants to and from the Southeast are not likely to be from, or remain in, the ranks of the unemployed. So we really do not know how a net change of Southeastern population would affect per capita personal income in this region without knowledge of the earnings status of all migrants before and after they migrate.

relative gains have been made, the dollar gap between Southeastern and national per capita income has not narrowed.

Changes in population are also important in analyzing per capita personal income. Population in the United States increased from 143,446,000 in 1947 to 181,062,000 in 1961, a total increase of 26.9 percent and an average annual increase of 1.8 percent. Population in the Southeast was 32,067,000 in 1947 and 39,465,000 in 1961. The growth of population in the Southeast during this period was 23.1 percent—an average annual growth rate of 1.5 percent, slightly less than for the ration as a whole. As a percent of United States total population, that of the Southeast declined from 22.4 percent in 1947 to 21.7 percent in 1961.

Timing and Durations

Table 2-2 shows the cyclical behavior of per capita personal income for the Southeast and the United States as a whole. The Southeast's series reached turning points on the same month as its counterpart in the United States, with the exception of the terminal trough of Cycle IV, at which time the Southeast lagged behind the nation by 1.0 month. Also, a direct comparison of turning points of this series with those of aggregate personal income indicated that both turned virtually simultaneously.

As was true of total personal income, the timing of turning points in per capita personal income in the Southeast conformed exceptionally well to the corresponding series in the nation as a whole.

The durations of cycles, and intracycle phases, in the Southeast were also very similar to those in the nation. All of the differences noted were due to the 1.0 month lag by the Southeastern series at the terminal trough of Cycle IV.

Amplitudes

Comparison of cyclical amplitudes indicates that per capita personal income was more sensitive to cyclical fluctua-

TABLE 2-2
TURNING POINTS, DURATIONS, AND AMPLITUDES OF CYCLES IN PER CAPITA PERSONAL INCOME, UNITED STATES AND SOUTHEAST

	Turning points			S.E. lead (−) or lag (+) (months)		Durations (months)			Amplitudes		
Cycle	Init. Trough	Peak	Term. Trough	Peak	Trough	Expan.	Contr.	Full Cycle	Expan.	Contr.	Full Cycle
Cycle I											
U.S.	(a)	9/48	8/49			(a)	11.0	(a)	(a)	−5.5	(a)
S.E.	(a)	9/48	8/49	0.0	0.0	(a)	11.0	(a)	(a)	−7.2	(a)
Cycle II											
U.S.	8/49	7/53	12/53			47.0	5.0	52.0	+27.2	−1.8	29.0
S.E.	8/49	7/53	12/53	0.0	0.0	47.0	5.0	52.0	+30.2	−1.3	31.5
Cycle III											
U.S.	12/53	8/57	12/57			44.0	4.0	48.0	+14.4	−1.9	16.3
S.E.	12/53	8/57	12/57	0.0	0.0	44.0	4.0	48.0	+17.3	−4.4	21.7
Cycle IV											
U.S.	12/57	7/60	1/61			31.0	6.0	37.0	+12.7	−2.2	14.9
S.E.	12/57	7/60	2/61	0.0	+1.0	31.0	7.0	38.0	+17.4	−5.1	22.5
Average[b]											
U.S.						40.7	5.0	45.7	+18.1	−2.0	20.1
S.E.				0.0	+0.3	40.7	5.3	46.0	+21.6	−3.6	25.2

[a] Data not available. [b] Each column averaged separately.
Source: See Appendix A.

tions in the Southeast than per capita personal income in the United States as a whole. The average amplitudes were larger in the Southeast during expansion, contraction and the complete cycle. The full-cycle and expansion amplitudes during all three complete cycles were larger for the Southeast; and during the contraction phase the amplitudes were larger in the Southeast with the exception of Cycle II, which was slightly smaller for the Southeast than for the nation.

Amplitudes of per capita personal income for the Southeast and the United States were smaller than those of total personal income for the expansion phase and for the full cycle, while the converse was true for the contraction phases.

CASH RECEIPTS FROM FARM MARKETINGS

Comparable monthly figures of cash receipts from farm marketings for the Southeast and the United States are available since 1950.[5] Since no turning points are observable in either series until 1953, the quantitative measures of cyclical fluctuations and comparative rates of change begin with 1953 figures.

Neither Southeastern nor United States cash receipts revealed an upward or downward trend over the period 1953-1961. After adjustment for seasonal variation the only movements observable were cyclical and erratic fluctuations. Cash receipts in the Southeast as a percentage of countrywide cash receipts varied from 19.0 percent to 20.8 percent, but this variation was not from the earliest to the latest period examined. Cash receipts, however, is a more important source of income in the Southeast than in the nation as a whole, a fact that becomes significant in evaluating the differential cyclical behavior of Southeastern and United States cash receipts.

[5] Raw data for cash receipts from farm marketings (hereafter referred to as cash receipts), for the United States and the Southeast are from U.S. Department of Agriculture, *Farm Income Situation*. See Appendix A for further description and evaluation.

TABLE 2-3
Turning Points, Durations, and Amplitudes of Cycles in Cash Receipts from Farm Marketings, United States and Southeast

Cycle	Turning points Init. Trough	Turning points Peak	Turning points Term. Trough	S.E. lead (−) or lag (+) (months) Peak	S.E. lead (−) or lag (+) (months) Trough	Durations (months) Expan.	Durations (months) Contr.	Durations (months) Full Cycle	Amplitudes Expan.	Amplitudes Contr.	Amplitudes Full Cycle
Cycle II											
U.S.	(a)	3/53	12/54	0.0	−1.0	(a)	21.0	(a)	(a)	− 5.8	(a)
S.E.	(a)	3/53	11/54			(a)	20.0	(a)	(a)	−13.6	(a)
Cycle III											
U.S.	12/54	10/56	9/57	0.0	0.0	22.0	11.0	33.0	+ 6.3	− 6.8	13.1
S.E.	11/54	10/56	9/57			23.0	11.0	34.0	+16.2	−19.1	35.3
Cycle IV											
U.S.	9/57	1/59	1/60	+6.0	0.0	16.0	12.0	28.0	+16.2	− 6.5	22.7
S.E.	9/57	7/59	1/60			22.0	6.0	28.0	+22.5	−12.3	34.8
Average[b]											
U.S.				+2.0	−0.3	19.0	11.5	30.5	+11.3	− 6.7	17.9
S.E.						22.5	8.5	31.0	+19.4	−15.7	35.1

[a] Data not available. [b] Each column averaged separately.
Source: See Appendix A.

Timing and Durations

Cash receipts in the Southeast lagged behind its counterpart in the United States by 6.0 months at the peak of Cycle IV, but there was no significant lead or lag at the troughs (Table 2-3). Comparison of turning points of cash receipts in the Southeast with personal income in the Southeast shows that the former tended to lead at peaks by several months. For the three peaks compared (Cycles II-IV), cash receipts led personal income by 4.0 months during Cycle II, and 10.0 months during Cycles III and IV. At the troughs the pattern was not clear, for cash receipts lagged behind personal income by 12.0 months in Cycle II, but led in Cycles III and IV by 3.0 months and 13.0 months, respectively.

No significant difference of average full-cycle duration occurred between the Southeast and the United States. However, there was a significant difference in the average duration of expansion and contraction between the two areas. The average expansion phase was 3.5 months longer and the average contraction phase 3.0 months shorter for the Southeast.

For the individual cycles, the only significant difference in duration occurred during Cycle IV. In this cycle the expansion phase was 6.0 months shorter for the Southeast than for the United States.

Full cycles of cash receipts in the Southeast were shorter on the average than the cycles of personal income in the Southeast. This was true also for the expansion phase; but the contraction phase in the Southeast was longer on the average for cash receipts than for personal income.

Amplitudes

A comparison of amplitudes of cash receipts for the Southeast and the United States (Table 2-3) indicates that this income series was considerably more sensitive to cyclical forces in the Southeast. The average amplitude was larger in the Southeast for the full-cycle, the expansion, and the contraction phases. It will be recalled that average amplitudes were larger in the Southeast for both personal income and per capita personal income; however, the magnitude of the difference between the Southeast and the United States was considerably greater for cash receipts than for the former two series. Averages correctly depict the relative behavior during the individual cycles; for no exceptions to the general pattern as revealed through the averages was noted upon examination of the individual cycles.

AVERAGE WEEKLY EARNINGS

Average weekly earnings cover only production workers in manufacturing industries, and these data are analyzed over the period 1953-1961.[6] Average weekly earnings in the Southeast have increased as a percentage of the national counterpart, although the absolute gap between the two has widened over the period under study.

Timing and Durations

Cyclical measures of average weekly earnings in the Southeast and the United States (Table 2-4) reveal a 4.0 month lag by Southeastern average weekly earnings at the peak of Cycle IV, which was the only significant difference in timing between the Southeast and the United States. The only significant difference of duration between the Southeast and United States also occurred in Cycle IV, when the expansion phase was 3.0 months longer and the contraction phase 3.0 months shorter for the Southeast than for the United States.

Amplitudes

The average amplitudes of expansion were slightly larger for the Southeast than for the United States; the opposite was true for contraction and full-cycle average amplitudes.

---

[6] Average weekly earnings of production workers in manufacturing are from data reported in U.S. Department of Labor, *Monthly Labor Review*. See Appendix A for further description and evaluation of data.

25

TABLE 2-4

Turning Points, Durations, and Amplitudes of Cycles in Average Weekly Earnings of Production Workers in Manufacturing, United States and Southeast

Cycle	Turning points			S.E. lead (−) or lag (+) (months)		Durations (months)			Amplitudes		
	Init. Trough	Peak	Term. Trough	Peak	Trough	Expan.	Contr.	Full Cycle	Expan.	Contr.	Full Cycle
Cycle II											
U.S.	(a)	4/53	4/54	0.0	−1.0	(a)	12.0	(a)	(a)	−1.4	(a)
S.E.	(a)	4/53	3/54			(a)	11.0	(a)	(a)	−2.0	(a)
Cycle III											
U.S.	4/54	8/57	3/58	0.0	+1.0	40.0	7.0	47.0	+15.5	−2.0	17.5
S.E.	3/54	8/57	4/58			41.0	8.0	49.0	+17.9	−1.3	19.2
Cycle IV											
U.S.	3/58	1/60	12/60	+4.0	+1.0	22.0	11.0	33.0	+11.4	−1.9	13.3
S.E.	4/58	5/60	1/61			25.0	8.0	33.0	+10.3	−1.0	11.3
Average[b]											
U.S.				+1.3	+0.3	31.0	9.0	40.0	+13.5	−2.0	15.4
S.E.						33.0	8.0	41.0	+14.1	−1.2	15.3

[a] Data not available.   [b] Each column averaged separately.
Source: See Appendix A.

The individual cycles did not show a very clear pattern. The expansion amplitude for the Southeast was larger during Cycle III, but smaller during Cycle IV than the corresponding national amplitudes. The same was true for full-cycle amplitudes. The contraction amplitude of Cycle II was larger for the Southeast than for the United States, but smaller for the Southeast during Cycles III and IV.

SUMMARY

Cyclical changes in personal income and in per capita personal income occurred at virtually the same time in the Southeast and in the United States; consequently, there was no significant difference in cyclical durations between the two areas. Amplitudes of cyclical fluctuations, however, were generally larger for the Southeast than for the United States.

Cash receipts from farm marketings and average weekly earnings of production workers in manufacturing industries each revealed one significant divergence in timing and in duration between the Southeast and the United States. Amplitudes of cyclical fluctuations show that the Southeast's cash receipts are considerably more sensitive than United States' cash receipts during periods of contraction and of expansion. The magnitude of the differences between the Southeast and the nation in amplitudes of cash receipts, plus the greater weight of this series in the Southeast, indicates that this source of income is probably the most important factor in accounting for the greater instability of Southeastern personal and per capita personal income.

Although no clear pattern of relative amplitudes emerged in average weekly earnings, the average amplitude was slightly larger for the Southeast during expansions and slightly smaller for the Southeast over the full cycle and contractions.

3

AGGREGATE AGRICULTURAL AND NONAGRICULTURAL EMPLOYMENT

*A*GRICULTURAL employment and nonagricultural employment, for the Southeast and the nation as a whole, could be summed to derive a total employment series but the results would be somewhat dubious, for these figures are estimated by two different agencies using different techniques. The two series are therefore examined individually.

Incompleteness of data limits the analysis of agricultural employment to only a twelve-year period. During the period 1950-1961 agricultural employment declined rapidly relative to total employment. And furthermore, the cyclical behavior of agricultural employment did not conform to other employment series during the postwar period. Consequently, there would be very little gained by further disaggregating this series. On the other hand, nonagricultural employment represented an increasing percentage of total employment during the period 1945-1961 and nonagricultural employment data are available by major industry divisions over the entire postwar period for both geographical areas. Disaggregation of the nonagricultural sector should give some insight into the relative cyclical stability (or instability) of the Southeast.[1]

AGRICULTURAL EMPLOYMENT

Comparable agricultural employment figures on a monthly basis, by state, are available only as far back as 1950. During this period only two cycles were discernible. Although the dates of these cycles did not conform to the reference-cycle dates, they occurred toward the end of the postwar period and are labeled Cycle III and Cyle IV (Table 3-1).

From 1950 to 1961, agricultural employment declined rapidly in the nation as a whole and even more rapidly in the Southeast. In 1950 agricultural employment in the United States was 9.9 million and represented 16.6 percent of total employment; by 1961 it had decreased to 7.0 million and represented only 10.5 percent of total United States employment. In the Southeast agricultural employment declined from 3.7 million to 2.4 million. The decrease in the twelve Southeastern states alone accounted for roughly 45 percent of the total decrease in the nation during this period. That Southeastern agricultural employment is declining more rapidly than in the nation as a whole is further indicated by the declining share of the Southeast in countrywide agricultural employment. In 1950 the Southeast had 37.4 percent of total agricultural employment; by 1961 it had only 33.9 percent.

[1] See Appendix A for sources, description, and evaluation of data used in this chapter.

TABLE 3-1

TURNING POINTS, DURATIONS, AND AMPLITUDES OF CYCLES IN AGRICULTURAL EMPLOYMENT, UNITED STATES AND SOUTHEAST

	Turning points			S.E. lead (−) or lag (+) (months)		Durations (months)			Amplitudes		
	Init.	Peak	Term.					Full			Full
Cycle	Trough	Peak	Trough	Peak	Trough	Expan.	Contr.	Cycle	Expan.	Contr.	Cycle
Cycle III											
U.S.	12/53	10/55	12/56			22.0	14.0	36.0	−4.9	−8.1	3.2
S.E.	12/53	10/55	12/56	0.0	0.0	22.0	14.0	36.0	−3.3	−11.3	8.3
Cycle IV											
U.S.	12/56	3/59	8/60			27.0	17.0	44.0	−1.4	−6.6	5.2
S.E.	12/56	3/59	8/60	0.0	0.0	27.0	17.0	44.0	−1.1	−10.6	9.5
Average[a]											
U.S.						24.5	15.5	40.0	−3.2	−7.4	4.2
S.E.				0.0	0.0	24.5	15.5	40.0	−2.2	−11.0	8.9

[a] Each column averaged separately.
Source: See Appendix A.

Timing and Durations

The turning points of agricultural employment in the Southeast were identical to those for the nation as a whole; consequently, the duration of the cycles and their phases are necessarily the same.

Amplitudes

Full-cycle amplitudes of agricultural employment were greater for the Southeast than for the nation as a whole. This was true of the average and of each of the individual cycles. Contraction amplitudes were also larger for the Southeast during both cycles. But the average expansion amplitude was smaller for the Southeast than for the United States. Expansion amplitudes were also smaller for the Southeast during each of the two cycles. But the smaller negative expansion amplitudes indicate that the positive cyclical influence, which generally prevails during expansion, was stronger for the Southeast than for the United States.

TOTAL NONAGRICULTURAL EMPLOYMENT

In contrast to agricultural employment, nonagricultural employment in the Southeast and in the United States has increased in absolute numbers and as a percentage of total employment. In 1945, there were 40.4 million employees in nonagricultural industries throughout the United States, representing 76.5 percent of the nation's total employment; by 1961 there were 54.1 million nonagricultural employees, representing 81.0 percent of total employment. For the Southeast, nonagricultural employment in 1945 was 6.3 million, 15.6 percent of total nonagricultural employment in the United States. In 1961 this figure was 9.6 million, 17.7 percent of national nonagricultural employment. The increase in nonagricultural employment from 1945 to 1961 was 51.2 percent for the Southeast and 33.9 percent for the United States.

Although specific-cycle turning points of nonagricultural employment in the United States have been established by the National Bureau of Economic Research, these dates were not used here since the data used in the present study clearly revealed the peaks and troughs. When plotted, the series for the United States and the Southeast were very smooth—particularly when compared with erratic agricultural employment (Table 3-2).

Timing and Durations

Timing of total nonagricultural employment in the Southeast was essentially the same as that of corresponding series in the United States. The only significant difference was a 4.0 month lag on the part of the Southeastern series at the peak of Cycle III.

Timing of nonagricultural employment in the Southeast relative to agricultural employment in the Southeast can be summed up briefly: There was total nonconformity between the two series. This was also true of these two employment series for the United States.[2]

Comparative durations show that the average expansion phase was slightly longer and the average contraction phase slightly shorter for the Southeast than for the United States. These differences were small, however. A review of the individual cycles indicates that expansion was 6.0 months longer and the contraction 5.0 months shorter for the Southeast than for the nation as a whole in Cycle III, but there was no significant difference during the other three cycles.

When the duration of this series for the Southeast was compared with the duration of agricultural employment, cycles and intracycle phases showed up much longer in the latter series, a characteristic that was more noticeable during the contraction phase than either the expansion phase or the full cycle.[3]

[2] Based on comparison over Cycles II and IV only.
[3] Based on comparison over Cycles II and IV only.

TABLE 3-2
TURNING POINTS, DURATIONS, AND AMPLITUDES OF CYCLES IN NONAGRICULTURAL EMPLOYMENT, UNITED STATES AND SOUTHEAST

Cycle	Turning points			S.E. lead (—) or lag (+) (months)		Durations (months)			Amplitudes		
	Init. Trough	Peak	Term. Trough	Peak	Trough	Expan.	Contr.	Full Cycle	Expan.	Contr.	Full Cycle
Cycle I											
U.S.	9/45	8/48	10/49	—1.0	0.0	35.0	14.0	49.0	+14.7	—4.4	19.1
S.E.	10/45	7/48	10/49			33.0	15.0	48.0	+15.8	—4.0	19.8
Cycle II											
U.S.	10/49	7/53	8/54	0.0	—2.0	45.0	13.0	58.0	+15.0	—3.5	18.5
S.E.	10/49	7/53	6/54			45.0	11.0	56.0	+17.9	—2.9	20.8
Cycle III											
U.S.	8/54	4/57	5/58	+4.0	—1.0	32.0	13.0	45.0	+ 8.2	—4.2	12.4
S.E.	6/54	8/57	4/58			38.0	8.0	46.0	+11.3	—2.2	13.5
Cycle IV											
U.S.	5/58	4/60	4/61	0.0	0.0	23.0	12.0	35.0	+ 6.4	—1.6	8.0
S.E.	4/58	4/60	4/61			24.0	12.0	36.0	+ 6.9	—0.6	7.5
Average[a]											
U.S.				+0.8	+0.8	33.8	13.0	46.8	+11.1	—3.4	14.5
S.E.						35.0	11.5	46.5	+13.0	—2.4	15.4

[a] Each column averaged separately.
Source: See Appendix A.

Amplitudes

Nonagricultural employment in the Southeast, as compared with its counterpart in the United States, revealed a greater average amplitude of expansion and a smaller average amplitude of contraction. Comparison of individual cycles shows that the averages closely depict the pattern of relative amplitudes; the only exception was a smaller full-cycle amplitude for the Southeast in Cycle IV.

Relative to the national performance, total nonagricultural employment in the Southeast was more stable than Southeastern agricultural employment. This was particularly true of the contraction phases. The relative stability of total nonagricultural employment in the Southeast during recessions is of particular interest, especially when one recalls that personal income in the Southeast was, on the average, more sensitive to recessions.

SUMMARY

Agricultural employment in the Southeast revealed cyclical peaks and troughs at the same time as peaks and troughs appeared in national agricultural employment. Consequently, cyclical durations were the same for both areas. Amplitudes of cyclical fluctuations, however, were larger for Southeastern agricultural employment than for the national counterpart.

Although Southeastern nonagricultural employment did not show turning points identical to those in the national series, there was overall very close conformity between the two areas. The only significant difference in timing was a 4.0 month lag at the peak of Cycle III on the part of the Southeastern series. This difference in timing was reflected in the relative duration of the intracycle phases of Cycle III. Although differences in duration were few and small, the average length of expansion was slightly longer and the average length of contraction was slightly shorter for Southeastern nonagricultural employment than for countrywide nonagricultural employment.

Amplitudes of fluctuations were generally larger for Southeastern nonagricultural employment during periods of expansion and smaller during periods of contraction, relative to their national counterpart. Over the full cycle, amplitudes were generally larger for the Southeast, a fact that indicates that the relatively stronger expansions in the Southeast more than offset the relatively weaker contractions in the Southeast.

4

COMMODITY-PRODUCING INDUSTRIES EMPLOYMENT

$\mathcal{T}$HE COMMODITY-PRODUCING sector of nonagricultural employment includes employment in mining, contract construction, and manufacturing industries.[1] Manufacturing employment is further disaggregated into durable- and nondurable-goods manufacturing, and a related series, average weekly hours of production workers in manufacturing, is examined. The breakdown of manufacturing employment is important because this type of employment represents more than three-fourths of total commodity-

[1] See Appendix A for sources, description, and evaluation of data used in this chapter.

producing employment and it is known that durable goods are more sensitive to cyclical swings than nondurable goods.

TOTAL COMMODITY-PRODUCING SECTOR

For the nation as a whole, total employment in the commodity-producing sector during the postwar years has increased slowly in absolute numbers and has actually declined as a percentage of total nonagricultural employment. In 1945, 17.5 million workers were employed in commodity-producing industries; by 1961 employment in this sector was 19.7 million. The proportion of total nonagricultural employment in commodity-producing industries was 43.3 percent in 1945; by 1961 it was only 36.4 percent.

Employment in the commodity-producing sector of the Southeast has also increased slowly, although faster than for the United States. Employment in these industries in the Southeast was 2.7 million in 1945 and 3.5 million in 1961. As a percentage of total Southeastern nonagricultural employment, employment in Southeastern commodity-producing industries decreased from 42.9 percent in 1945 to 36.8 percent in 1961. The proportion of nationwide commodity-producing employment in the Southeast ranged from 15.5 percent in 1945 to 17.9 percent in 1961. In this respect, the Southeast has made some relative gain on the nation as a whole.

Timing

A comparison of timing reveals no significant difference between the Southeast and the United States with respect to average lead or lag (Table 4-1). The Southeast lagged behind the nation at peaks an average of 1.5 months and lagged behind at troughs an average of 3.3 months. Examination of the individual cycles shows only one significant difference in timing: a 5.0 month lag by the Southeast at the peak of Cycle III.

Cyclical turning points in employment in the com-

TABLE 4-1
TURNING POINTS, DURATIONS, AND AMPLITUDES OF CYCLES IN THE COMMODITY-PRODUCING SECTOR, UNITED STATES AND SOUTHEAST

Cycle	Turning points			S.E. lead (−) or lag (+) (months)		Durations (months)			Amplitudes		
	Init. Trough	Peak	Term. Trough	Peak	Trough	Expan.	Contr.	Full Cycle	Expan.	Contr.	Full Cycle
Cycle I											
U.S.	10/45	7/48	10/49			33.0	15.0	48.0	+19.0	− 9.5	28.5
S.E.	11/45	6/48	10/49	−1.0	0.0	31.0	16.0	47.0	+20.3	−11.4	31.7
Cycle II											
U.S.	10/49	7/53	8/54			45.0	13.0	58.0	+21.0	− 8.8	29.8
S.E.	10/49	7/53	8/54	0.0	0.0	45.0	13.0	58.0	+19.5	− 7.1	26.6
Cycle III											
U.S.	8/54	2/57	6/58			30.0	16.0	46.0	+ 8.2	−10.1	18.3
S.E.	8/54	7/57	5/58	+5.0	−1.0	35.0	10.0	45.0	+10.3	− 4.9	15.2
Cycle IV											
U.S.	6/58	2/60	2/61			20.0	12.0	32.0	+ 7.5	− 5.8	13.3
S.E.	5/58	4/60	4/61	+2.0	+2.0	23.0	12.0	35.0	+ 7.3	− 3.5	10.8
Average[a]											
U.S.						32.0	14.0	46.0	+13.9	− 8.55	22.5
S.E.				+1.5	+0.25	33.5	12.8	46.3	+14.4	− 6.72	21.1

[a] Each column averaged separately.
Source: See Appendix A.

modity-producing sector occurred at about the same time as those in total nonagricultural employment, a characteristic true of the series for both the Southeast and the United States.

Durations

The comparison of durations indicates that the average lengths of the full cycles, the expansions, and the contractions were roughly the same for the Southeast and the nation. Of the individual cycles, only Cycles III and IV revealed significant divergencies in duration between the Southeast and the United States. In Cycle III, the expansion phase was 5.0 months longer and the contraction phase 6.0 months shorter for the Southeast, but the difference for the complete cycle was only 1.0 month. During Cycle IV the expansion phase and the full cycle were both 3.0 months longer in the Southeast, but this cycle showed no difference between duration of the contraction phases of Southeastern and national commodity-producing employment.

The average durations of cycles in employment in the commodity-producing sector in the Southeast were virtually the same as those of total nonagricultural employment.

Amplitudes

Comparison of amplitudes for the Southeast and United States in Table 3-3 indicates that the average amplitudes of employment in commodity-producing industries in the Southeast were larger during the expansion phase and smaller during the contraction phase than the corresponding amplitudes for the United States, the same relative behavior noted for total nonagricultural employment. However, unlike total nonagricultural employment, the average full-cycle amplitude of this series was smaller for the Southeast than for the nation as a whole.

Full-cycle amplitudes were smaller for the Southeast than for the United States during three cycles (Cycles II-IV), and larger during one (Cycle I). No set pattern of relative expansion amplitudes emerged; the Southeast had a larger amplitude during two cycles (Cycles I and III) and a smaller amplitude during two cycles (Cycles II and IV), while the contraction amplitudes were smaller in the Southeast during three cycles (Cycles II-IV) and larger during one cycle (Cycle I).

Amplitudes of expansion, contraction, and the full cycle were generally larger for employment in the commodity-producing sector than for the total nonagricultural employment series.

MINING

Employment in mining industries declined during the postwar period and the decline has been more noticeable in recent years. Employment in this industry is small relative to total employment in commodity-producing industries.

In 1945 there were 836,000 workers in mining throughout the United States. This represented 4.8 percent of total employment in the commodity-producing sector. By 1961 employment in mining industries had fallen to 667,000, representing only 3.4 percent of employment in the commodity-producing sector.

Mining employment in the Southeast also declined during the postwar years. The decline was from 271,000 employees in 1945 to 190,000 in 1961. These figures represented 10.0 percent of employment in Southeastern commodity-producing industries in 1945 and 5.4 percent in 1961. Southeastern mining employment as a proportion of national mining employment was 32.4 percent in 1945 and 28.5 percent in 1961.

Timing

Mining employment in the Southeast turned simultaneously with the corresponding series in the United States at all four peaks and at the troughs. The only significant difference in timing between the two cognate series was a

TABLE 4-2
Turning Points, Durations, and Amplitudes of Cycles in Mining Employment,
United States and Southeast

	Turning points			S.E. lead (—) or lag (+) (months)		Durations (months)			Amplitudes		
	Init.		Term.					Full			Full
Cycle	Trough	Peak	Trough	Peak	Trough	Expan.	Contr.	Cycle	Expan.	Contr.	Cycle
Cycle I											
U.S.	10/45	9/48	10/49	0.0	0.0	35.0	13.0	48.0	+19.1	—20.8	39.9
S.E.	10/45	9/48	10/49			35.0	13.0	48.0	+19.0	—27.6	46.6
Cycle II											
U.S.	10/49	7/53	9/54	0.0	0.0	45.0	14.0	59.0	+ 5.8	—11.1	16.9
S.E.	10/49	7/53	9/54			45.0	14.0	59.0	+ 0.3	—13.7	14.0
Cycle III											
U.S.	9/54	7/57	6/58	0.0	+1.0	34.0	11.0	45.0	+ 9.0	—12.7	21.7
S.E.	9/54	7/57	7/58			34.0	12.0	46.0	+15.8	—14.5	30.3
Cycle IV											
U.S.	6/58	4/60	4/61	0.0	—3.0	22.0	12.0	34.0	— 2.4	— 8.1	5.7
S.E.	7/58	4/60	1/61			21.0	9.0	30.0	— 5.8	— 6.3	0.5
Average[a]											
U.S.				0.0	—0.5	34.0	12.5	46.5	+ 7.9	—13.2	21.1
S.E.						33.8	12.0	45.8	+ 7.3	—15.5	22.9

[a] Each column averaged separately.
Source: See Appendix A.

3.0 month lead by Southeastern mining employment at the terminal trough of Cycle IV (Table 4-2).

Employment in mining in the Southeast also conformed closely to the commodity-producing series. Only two significant divergencies in dates of turning points were observed; the mining series turned 3.0 months later at the peak of Cycle I and 3.0 months earlier at the terminal trough of Cycle IV than the commodity-producing series.

Differences between the Southeast and the United States in the timing of cycles in mining employment were fewer than for commodity-producing employment. But both series in the Southeast conformed very well with the United States as a whole.

Durations

No significant difference between the average length of these cycles or intracycle phases for the Southeast and the nation as a whole was observed. A review of the separate cycles, however, showed that Cycle IV was 4.0 months shorter in the Southeast and that the contraction phase of this cycle was 3.0 months shorter in the Southeast than in the United States.

The average durations of the expansion phase, the contraction phase, and the full cycle of mining employment in the Southeast were virtually the same as those of employment in Southeastern commodity-producing establishments. Comparison of the individual cycles of mining and commodity-producing employment indicated that the only significant differences between the two series occurred during Cycle IV, when the contraction phase was 3.0 months shorter for mining than for the parent sector, and the full-cycle duration was 5.0 months shorter for mining than for the parent sector.

Amplitudes

The average full-cycle amplitude was slightly larger for the Southeast than for the United States. The average contraction amplitude was also larger for the Southeast, but the expansion amplitude for the Southeast was slightly smaller. This behavior in mining employment is opposite to the relative behavior of average amplitudes noted in the analysis of the commodity-producing sector.

With respect to the relative behavior during the individual cycles, the pattern is not clear for full-cycle amplitudes. The full-cycle amplitudes were smaller for the Southeast than for the United States during two cycles and larger during two cycles. The expansion amplitude was smaller in the Southeast for three cycles (although the difference in cycle relatives was only 0.1 for Cycle I) and larger for one cycle. The contraction phase was the reverse: during three cycles the amplitude of contraction was larger and during one cycle it was smaller for the Southeast than for the United States.

This series fluctuated quite differently from the parent series during the intracycle phases. Mining employment was more sensitive to cyclical fluctuations during periods of contraction than during periods of expansion, while the opposite was true of employment in commodity-producing industries.

CONTRACT CONSTRUCTION

In contrast to mining, employment figures in contract construction indicated that this was a rapidly growing industry throughout the United States. In 1945, 1.1 million persons were employed in nationwide contract construction; by 1961 employment in these industries had increased to 2.8 million. As a proportion of total employment in commodity-producing industries, contract construction employment increased from 6.5 percent in 1945 to 14.0 percent in 1961.

The increase in contract construction employment in the Southeast was from 227,000 in 1945 to 572,000 in 1961. These figures represented, respectively, 8.4 percent and 16.3 percent of total employment in Southeastern commodity-producing industries. The Southeast's share of nationwide employment in contract construction was 20.1 percent in 1945 and 20.7 percent in 1961. Thus, the Southeast has barely maintained its proportion of employment in contract construction over the postwar period.

Timing

The differences in the timing of cycles in this series for the Southeast and its counterpart for the United States, as revealed through average leads and lags, were quite small (Table 4-3). But these averages conceal some larger differences in timing that occurred during the individual cycles. The Southeast lagged behind the nation at the initial trough of Cycle I by 5.0 months, and led the nation by 6.0 months at the peak. In Cycle II the Southeast lagged behind the United States by 7.0 months at the terminal trough, and during Cycle III the Southeast lagged behind at the peak by 7.0 months.

Turning points of contract construction employment in the Southeast were significantly different from those of employment in Southeastern mining on most occasions. At least one significant difference in the turning points was observed in each of the four cycles.

Contract construction employment in the Southeast showed less similarity to its counterpart in the United States, with respect to timing, than either mining employment or employment in the commodity-producing sector of the Southeast when compared with their corresponding series in the United States.

Durations

The comparison of average durations of expansions, contractions, and full cycles was also misleading. The differences in average durations between the Southeast and the United States were insignificant, but comparisons within each cycle revealed significant differences in duration between the Southeast and the United States in every cycle except

TABLE 4-3
TURNING POINTS, DURATIONS, AND AMPLITUDES OF CYCLES IN CONTRACT CONSTRUCTION EMPLOYMENT, UNITED STATES AND SOUTHEAST

Cycle	Turning points			S.E. lead (−) or lag (+) (months)		Durations (months)			Amplitudes	
	Init. Trough	Peak	Term. Trough	Peak	Trough	Expan.	Contr.	Full Cycle	Expan. Contr.	Full Cycle
Cycle I										
U.S.	5/45	12/48	6/49	−6.0	0.0	43.0	6.0	49.0	+60.4 — 4.5	64.9
S.E.	10/45	6/48	6/49			32.0	12.0	44.0	+55.8 — 7.5	63.3
Cycle II										
U.S.	6/49	2/53	1/54	−1.0	+7.0	44.0	11.0	55.0	+21.0 — 2.2	23.2
S.E.	6/49	1/53	8/54			43.0	19.0	62.0	+36.2 —14.1	50.3
Cycle III										
U.S.	1/54	3/57	2/58	+7.0	0.0	38.0	11.0	49.0	+13.6 — 8.4	22.0
S.E.	8/54	10/57	2/58			38.0	4.0	42.0	+16.5 — 3.7	20.2
Cycle IV										
U.S.	2/58	7/60	4/61	−2.0	0.0	29.0	10.0	39.0	+ 4.5 — 5.2	9.7
S.E.	2/58	5/60	4/61			27.0	11.0	38.0	+ 6.4 — 6.0	12.4
Average[a]										
U.S.				−0.5	+1.8	38.5	9.5	48.0	+24.9 — 5.1	30.0
S.E.						35.0	11.5	46.5	+28.7 — 7.8	36.6

[a] Each column averaged separately.
Source: See Appendix A.

Cycle IV. The expansion phase of Cycle I was 11.0 months shorter, the contraction phase 6.0 months longer, and the full cycle 5.0 months shorter for the Southeast than for the nation. In Cycle II, significant differences were noted during the contraction and the full cycle: the period of contraction of this cycle lasted 8.0 months longer in the Southeast than for the United States. And both the contraction phase and the full cycle were both 7.0 months shorter for the Southeastern states during Cycle III.

Employment in Southeastern contract construction did not conform to employment in Southeastern mining or commodity-producing establishments with respect to the length of cycles and intracycle phases. Although no significant difference in the average cycle duration of these three series was observed, the individual cycles were quite different in duration.

Nor did employment in contract construction for the Southeast reveal as close a relationship, with respect to duration, to the corresponding series in the United States as mining and the commodity-producing sector did to their respective counterparts in the nation as a whole.

Amplitudes

The average amplitudes of expansion, contraction, and the full cycle were larger for the Southeast than for the United States. The amplitudes for Cycle II were considerably larger for the Southeast. Stated in cycle relatives, the expansion amplitude of this cycle was 36.2 for the Southeast compared with 21.0 for the United States; the contraction amplitude was 14.1 for the Southeast and only 2.2 for the United States; and the full-cycle amplitude for the Southeast was 50.3 compared with 23.2 for the United States. The expansion phase of Cycle I was an exception to the average behavior; for the amplitude of this expansion phase was smaller for the Southeast than for the United States. And the amplitude of contraction of Cycle III was smaller for the Southeast than for the United States, which is also an exception to the average behavior. During two cycles (Cycles I and III) full-cycle amplitudes were smaller for the Southeast than for the United States, but only slightly so.

This series for the Southeast was considerably more sensitive to cyclical forces than was its counterpart for the nation as a whole. Relative to their respective national counterparts, employment in contract construction was also more sensitive than either employment in mining or employment in the commodity-producing industries. But it more closely paralleled the relative behavior of mining than the relative behavior of the parent sector.

MANUFACTURING

Manufacturing employment is the third major component of the commodity-producing sector to be analyzed in this chapter. Employment in manufacturing during the postwar years increased faster than in mining but slower than in contract construction for the United States as a whole and for the Southeast. It also represented a larger proportion of employment in the commodity-producing sector than did the combination of mining and contract construction.

In 1945 employment in United States manufacturing was 15.5 million, representing 88.7 percent of total employment in the commodity-producing sector. In 1961 there were 16.3 million workers in manufacturing, representing 82.6 percent of commodity-producing employment.

There were 2.2 million employees in Southeastern manufacturing industries in 1945, representing 81.7 percent of total employment in Southeastern commodity-producing industries, and in 1961 this figure was 2.8 million, representing 78.3 percent of commodity-producing workers. During the period under study the Southeast increased its share of the nation's manufacturing employment from 14.3 percent in 1945 to 16.9 percent in 1961.

Timing

The average number of months the Southeast led or lagged the United States at turning points was insignificant (see Table 4-4). Examination of the individual cycles, however, shows two significant differences in timing, both occurring in Cycle I. The Southeast lagged behind the United States at the peak of this cycle by 5.0 months and led the United States at the terminal trough by 4.0 months.

Manufacturing employment in the Southeast turned more synchronously with the parent series than with either mining or contract construction employment, though there were two significant differences between turning points of the peaks (Cycles I and III) of manufacturing employment as compared with the commodity-producing series. The differences in timing between manufacturing employment and the parent sector were not consistent enough to indicate that the former tended to lead or lag behind the latter at turning points. This was also true of the difference between turning points of manufacturing employment and the two companion series, mining and contract construction employment.

Relative to their respective national counterparts, employment in manufacturing in the Southeast revealed fewer significant differences of turning points than Southeastern employment in contract construction, but more significant differences than either employment in Southeastern mining or the commodity-producing sector.

Durations

One significant difference appeared between the average duration of the contraction phases in the Southeast and the United States, but no significant difference was observed between Southeast and national averages of expansion or full-cycle durations. The average length of contraction, however, was 3.0 months shorter for the Southeast than for the United States.

For the individual cycles, significant differences in dura-

TABLE 4-4
TURNING POINTS, DURATIONS, AND AMPLITUDES OF CYCLES IN MANUFACTURING EMPLOYMENT, UNITED STATES AND SOUTHEAST

Cycle	Turning points			S.E. lead (−) or lag (+) (months)		Durations (months)			Amplitudes		
	Init. Trough	Peak	Term. Trough	Peak	Trough	Expan.	Contr.	Full Cycle	Expan.	Contr.	Full Cycle
Cycle I											
U.S.	10/45	1/48	11/49	+5.0	−4.0	27.0	22.0	49.0	+14.6	−10.2	24.8
S.E.	11/45	6/48	7/49			31.0	13.0	44.0	+15.3	−10.9	26.2
Cycle II											
U.S.	11/49	7/53	8/54	0.0	0.0	44.0	13.0	57.0	+22.8	−10.3	33.1
S.E.	7/49	7/53	8/54			48.0	13.0	61.0	+19.9	− 5.6	25.5
Cycle III											
U.S.	8/54	3/57	5/58	+1.0	0.0	31.0	14.0	45.0	+ 7.4	−10.1	17.5
S.E.	8/54	4/57	5/58			32.0	13.0	45.0	+ 8.6	− 4.5	13.1
Cycle IV											
U.S.	5/58	2/60	2/61	+2.0	0.0	21.0	12.0	33.0	+ 8.3	− 6.2	14.5
S.E.	5/58	4/60	2/61			23.0	10.0	33.0	+ 9.2	− 3.2	12.4
Average[a]											
U.S.				+2.0	−1.0	30.8	15.3	46.0	+13.3	− 9.2	22.5
S.E.						33.5	12.3	45.8	+13.3	− 6.1	19.3

[a] Each column averaged separately.
Source: See Appendix A.

tion were noted in Cycles I and II. For Cycle I the expansion phase was 4.0 months longer for the Southeast than for the United States, the contraction phase 9.0 months shorter, and the full duration 5.0 months shorter. In both full duration and expansion Cycle II lasted 4.0 months longer in the Southeast than in the nation; however, durations of contraction were the same in both areas for this cycle.

The average durations of full cycles and of intracycle phases of Southeastern manufacturing employment were quite similar to those of the parent sector and to those of the two companion series.

Durations of cycles and intracycle phases of Southeast manufacturing employment were more similar to those of national manufacturing employment than were durations of Southeast contract construction compared with their national counterparts. However, durations of cycles and intracycle phases of Southeast mining employment and of employment in the Southeast parent sector were more similar to their national counterparts than were Southeast manufacturing employment.

Amplitudes

The average amplitudes were smaller for the Southeast than for the nation during the contraction phase and the full cycle, but the average amplitudes were the same for the Southeast and the United States for the expansion phase.

Comparison of amplitudes for the Southeast and the United States during the individual cycles reveals that expansion amplitudes were larger for the Southeast during three of the four cycles, but only slightly so. Contraction amplitudes for the Southeast were smaller during the last three cycles, and during the first cycle only slightly larger than the United States. The full-cycle amplitudes were smaller for the Southeast during three cycles and larger during one cycle. Thus, the averages closely depict the behavior of amplitudes for the Southeast as compared with the nation as a whole.

Of the three major components of the commodity-producing sector, manufacturing employment amplitudes appear to be closer in magnitude to those of the parent series than to either mining or contract construction.

Overall, Southeast manufacturing employment was more stable than its national counterpart, whereas Southeast mining employment, contract construction employment, and employment in the parent sector were less stable than their respective national counterparts.

DURABLE-GOODS MANUFACTURING

Employment in durable-goods manufacturing for the nation as a whole declined during the period 1953-1961 in absolute numbers and as a percentage of total manufacturing employment. In 1953 there were 10.1 million employees in durable-goods manufacturing. This represented 57.6 percent of total United States manufacturing. The number of workers in this industry declined to 9.0 million in 1961 and at that time represented 55.6 percent of total employment in United States manufacturing.

The trend was the opposite for the ten Southeastern states included in this series. Total durable-goods manufacturing employment for these states was 822,000 in 1953 and 943,000 in 1961. These figures represented 32.1 percent and 34.3 percent of total manufacturing employment in the Southeast for 1953 and 1961, respectively. Durable-goods employment for the ten Southeastern states also increased as a percentage of nationwide durable-goods employment, increasing from 8.1 percent in 1953 to 10.4 percent in 1961.

Timing

A 5.0 month lag by the Southeastern series at the peak of Cycle III was the only significant difference in timing of employment in durable-goods manufacturing for the Southeast and the nation (Table 4-5).

Southeastern employment in durable-goods manufacturing turned at approximately the same time as Southeastern

TABLE 4-5
Turning Points, Durations, and Amplitudes of Cycles in Durable-Goods Manufacturing Employment, United States and Southeast

	Turning points			S.E. lead (−) or lag (+) (months)		Durations (months)			Amplitudes		
	Init. Trough	Peak	Term. Trough	Peak	Trough	Expan.	Contr.	Full Cycle	Expan.	Contr.	Full Cycle
Cycle II											
U.S.	(a)	4/53	8/54	0.0	−2.0	(a)	16.0	(a)	(a)	−14.1	(a)
S.E.	(a)	4/53	6/54			(a)	14.0	(a)	(a)	− 8.1	(a)
Cycle III											
U.S.	8/54	2/57	5/58	+5.0	0.0	30.0	15.0	45.0	+11.3	−14.5	25.8
S.E.	6/54	7/57	5/58			37.0	10.0	47.0	+14.6	− 7.6	22.2
Cycle IV											
U.S.	5/58	2/60	2/61	+2.0	0.0	21.0	12.0	33.0	+11.5	− 9.2	20.7
S.E.	5/58	4/60	2/61			23.0	10.0	33.0	+17.1	− 6.3	23.4
Average[b]											
U.S.				+2.3	−0.67	25.5	13.5	39.0	+11.4	−11.9	23.3
S.E.						30.0	10.0	40.0	+15.9	− 7.0	22.8

[a] Data not available.   [b] Each column averaged separately.
Source: See Appendix A.

employment in manufacturing at troughs, but there were two significant differences in timing at peaks: durable-goods manufacturing led by 3.0 months at the peak of Cycle II and lagged behind by 3.0 months at the peaks of Cycles II and III.[2]

Relative to the corresponding series in the nation, durable-goods manufacturing employment in the Southeast revealed one significant divergence in timing during Cycles II-IV, but no significant difference emerged during these cycles for total manufacturing employment.

Durations

The average durations of expansion and average durations of contraction were significantly different for the Southeast and the United States. The average expansion phase was 4.5 months longer for the Southeast and the contraction phase 3.5 months shorter for the Southeast than for the United States. But there was relatively little difference between the average durations of the full cycle.

For the individual cycles, the durations differed significantly only during Cycle III; in this cycle the expansion was 7.0 months longer and the contraction 5.0 months shorter in the Southeast than in the United States.

For the Southeast, this series did not conform to the manufacturing series with respect to the duration of the intracycle phases of Cycle III. Expansion in Southeastern durable-goods manufacturing employment was 5.0 months longer and contraction 3.0 months shorter than for total Southeastern manufacturing employment during this cycle.

Based on Cycles III and IV, cycle and intracycle durations of employment in Southeastern durable-goods manufacturing employment did not conform as well to the corresponding series in the nation as did Southeastern manufacturing employment relative to its national counterpart.

[2] Comparison of employment in durable-goods manufacturing with total manufacturing employment is based on Cycles II-IV only.

Amplitudes

The average full-cycle amplitude was slightly smaller for the Southeast than for the United States; the average expansion amplitude was larger and the average contraction amplitude was much smaller for the Southeast than for the nation as a whole.

For the individual cycles the full-cycle amplitude was smaller for the Southeast during Cycle III and larger during Cycle IV. During Cycle III and Cycle IV, the expansion amplitude was larger for the Southeast than for the United States. All three contraction amplitudes were smaller for the Southeast than for the United States.

This series in the Southeast, relative to the national performance, was not quite so stable as was Southeastern total manufacturing employment, relative to its national counterpart.

Employment in Southeastern durable-goods industries was also more sensitive to cyclical swings than Southeastern manufacturing employment, as revealed from a direct comparison of their amplitudes.

NONDURABLE-GOODS MANUFACTURING

Employment in nondurable-goods manufacturing in the United States, like that in durable-goods manufacturing, declined in absolute numbers over the period 1953-1961. But unlike durable-goods manufacturing employment, nondurable-goods employment increased as a percentage of total manufacturing employment.

In 1953 there were 7.4 million workers in nondurable-goods manufacturing in the United States, representing 42.4 percent of total manufacturing employment. In 1961 employment was 7.2 million and represented 44.4 percent of total manufacturing employment.

In the Southeast, employment in nondurable-goods manufacturing increased slightly in absolute numbers and as a percent of total employment in Southeastern manufacturing.

Employees in nondurable-goods manufacturing in the Southeast numbered 1.4 million in 1953. This represented 53.6 percent of total Southeastern manufacturing employment. In 1961, 1.5 million workers were employed in nondurable-goods manufacturing, representing 54.1 percent of manufacturing employment in the Southeast. The Southeast also gained slightly, relative to the nation, in this type of employment. In 1953 the Southeast had 18.5 percent of nationwide employment in nondurable-goods manufacturing; by 1961 this region had 20.6 percent of nondurable-goods employment.

Timing

Employment in nondurable-goods manufacturing for the Southeast and the United States turned at the troughs almost simultaneously (Table 4-6). This was also true of the peaks of Cycles II and IV, but the Southeast lagged behind the United States by 14.0 months at the peak of Cycle III. This is the largest difference in timing noted in any series thus far. As a consequence of this rather large lag and a 1.0 month lag at the peak of Cycle IV, the average lag at peaks was 5.0 months, also the largest average divergence noted so far.

Nondurable-goods and durable-goods manufacturing employment behaved more alike than nondurable-goods and total manufacturing employment, insofar as the timing of the Southeastern series relative to the nation was concerned. (This is, of course, based on comparison of Cycles II-IV only.) Both durable-goods and nondurable-goods employment revealed considerable lags at the peak of Cycle III. The lag was much longer, however, for employment in nondurable-goods manufacturing.

Comparison of total manufacturing, durable-goods manufacturing, and nondurable-goods manufacturing employment (all in the Southeast) showed that, in regard to timing, nondurable goods conformed better with the parent series than with durable goods.

TABLE 4-6
TURNING POINTS, DURATIONS, AND AMPLITUDES OF CYCLES IN NONDURABLE-GOODS
MANUFACTURING EMPLOYMENT, UNITED STATES AND SOUTHEAST

Cycle	Turning points			S.E. lead (—) or lag (+) (months)		Durations (months)			Amplitudes		
	Init. Trough	Peak	Term. Trough	Peak	Trough	Expan.	Contr.	Full Cycle	Expan.	Contr.	Full Cycle
Cycle II											
U.S.	(a)	7/53	8/54			(a)	13.0	(a)	(a)	—4.7	(a)
S.E.	(a)	7/53	7/54	0.0	—1.0	(a)	12.0	(a)	(a)	—3.3	(a)
Cycle III											
U.S.	8/54	2/56	5/58			18.0	27.0	45.0	+3.9	—5.1	9.0
S.E.	7/54	4/57	4/58	+14.0	—1.0	33.0	12.0	45.0	+6.4	—2.3	8.7
Cycle IV											
U.S.	5/58	4/60	2/61			23.0	10.0	33.0	+4.3	—2.6	6.9
S.E.	4/58	5/60	2/61	+1.0	0.0	25.0	9.0	34.0	+7.4	—1.8	9.2
Average[b]											
U.S.						20.5	18.5	39.0	+4.1	—3.9	8.0
S.E.				+5.0	—0.7	29.0	10.5	39.5	+6.9	—2.1	9.0

[a] Data not available.   [b] Each column averaged separately.
Source: See Appendix A.

Durations

The durations of these cycles and cycle phases were very similar for the Southeast and the United States, except for the effects of the 14.0 month lag at the peak of Cycle III. And, even so, differences in full-cycle duration for the individual cycles and the average were insignificant. Primarily as a result of the long lag of the Southeast in Cycle III, the expansion phase in the Southeast was 15.0 months longer and the contraction phase 15.0 months shorter than for the United States. The average expansion phase was 8.5 months longer and the average contraction phase was 8.0 months shorter for the Southeast than for the United States.

The relative behavior of this series in the Southeast was not as similar to the corresponding series in the United States as were the employment series for durable-goods manufacturing and total manufacturing.

Amplitudes

The average amplitude of full cycles was slightly larger for the Southeast than for the United States. For the individual cycles, it was larger for Cycle IV, but slightly smaller for Cycle III. The average expansion amplitude was also larger for the Southeast, as was true for the individual cycles as well. On the other hand, contraction amplitudes were smaller for the Southeast, by all measures.

All amplitudes for this series were smaller than those of durable-goods manufacturing or total manufacturing in the Southeast. This was also true for the United States.

The relative behavior of this series in the Southeast to its counterpart in the nation was very similar to the relative behavior of Southeastern total manufacturing employment to the corresponding national series.

AVERAGE WEEKLY HOURS OF PRODUCTION WORKERS IN MANUFACTURING

Average weekly hours have not changed appreciably for the Southeast or for the United States since 1953. For the

United States, annual average weekly hours ranged from 40.7 to 39.2. The range was roughly the same for the Southeast. Annual average weekly hours for the Southeast ranged from 40.7 to 39.3. For both the United States and the Southeast the highest annual average occurred in 1955 and in 1958. The annual average was 40.5 for the Southeast and the United States in 1953; in 1961 it was 40.1 for the Southeast and 39.8 for the United States.

Timing

Turning points of this series in the Southeast and the United States occurred almost simultaneously. On no occasion was there a significant difference in timing between the two areas (Table 4-7).

This series in the Southeast behaved more like its national counterpart than did any of the manufacturing employment series.

Average weekly hours in the Southeast and in the United States tended to lead turns in total manufacturing employment (based on a comparison of Cycles II-IV of both series). Significant leads occurred at the peaks of all three cycles and the trough of Cycle II. At the peak of Cycle II average weekly hours turned 3.0 months earlier than total manufacturing employment in the Southeast and the United States. In Cycle III the lead was 15.0 months for the Southeast and 16.0 months for the United States. And for Cycle IV the lead was 11.0 months for the Southeast and 9.0 months for the United States.

Durations

At no time was there more than 2.0 months difference between the duration in the Southeast and the nation as a whole. A comparison of only the last two cycles and the contraction phase of Cycle II of total manufacturing with the average weekly hours series shows that both series in the Southeast were very similar to their counterparts in the nation during the period studied. Comparison of the average

TABLE 4-7
TURNING POINTS, DURATIONS, AND AMPLITUDES OF CYCLES IN AVERAGE WEEKLY HOURS OF PRODUCTION WORKERS IN MANUFACTURING, UNITED STATES AND SOUTHEAST

Cycle	Turning points				S.E. lead (−) or lag (+) (months)		Durations (months)			Amplitudes		
	Init. Trough	Peak	Term. Trough		Peak	Trough	Expan.	Contr.	Full Cycle	Expan.	Contr.	Full Cycle
Cycle II												
U.S.	(a)	4/53	4/54		0.0	+1.0	(a)	12.0	(a)	(a)	−3.7	(a)
S.E.	(a)	4/53	5/54				(a)	13.0	(a)	(a)	−4.0	(a)
Cycle III												
U.S.	4/54	11/55	4/58		+2.0	0.0	19.0	29.0	48.0	+3.5	−5.5	9.0
S.E.	5/54	1/56	4/58				20.0	27.0	47.0	+3.8	−5.8	9.6
Cycle IV												
U.S.	4/58	5/59	12/60		0.0	+1.0	13.0	19.0	32.0	+4.8	−4.3	9.1
S.E.	4/58	5/59	1/61				13.0	20.0	33.0	+5.9	−3.5	9.2
Average[b]												
U.S.					+0.7	+0.7	16.0	24.0	40.0	+4.2	−4.9	9.1
S.E.							16.5	23.5	40.0	+4.9	−4.7	9.4

[a] Data not available.   [b] Each column averaged separately.
Source: See Appendix A.

weekly hours to total manufacturing employment shows, however, that there was considerable difference between the durations of the contraction phases and expansion phases of these two series. This was true for both the Southeast and the United States. The expansion phase of Cycle III was 12.0 months shorter for average weekly hours than for manufacturing employment in the Southeast and in the United States. The contraction phase of Cycle II was 14.0 months longer in the Southeast and 15.0 months longer in the United States for average weekly hours than for total manufacturing employment. During Cycle IV the expansion phase of average weekly hours was 10.0 months and 8.0 months shorter for the Southeast and the United States, respectively, than the expansion phase for total manufacturing employment. The contraction of this cycle was 10.0 months longer for the Southeast and 7.0 months longer for the United States for the average weekly hours series than for the total manufacturing employment series. The only significant difference in the durations of full cycles was for the United States. The full-cycle duration of Cycle III of average weekly hours was 3.0 months longer than for total manufacturing employment in the United States.

Amplitudes

The average amplitudes were larger for the Southeast than for the nation during the expansion phase and the full cycle. But the average contraction amplitude was smaller for the Southeast. The difference in all cases was very small.

During both cycles the amplitudes of expansion were slightly larger for the Southeast. This was also true of the full-cycle amplitudes. During the three contraction phases, the amplitudes for the Southeast were smaller for two cycles and larger for the other. Again, it should be pointed out that these differences were all very small.

Compared with the relative behavior of employment in manufacturing, the behavior of average weekly hours was slightly more sensitive in the Southeast. But this series is apparently less sensitive to cyclical forces because amplitudes of average weekly hours were smaller than those of manufacturing employment. This holds for the series in the United States as well as for the Southeast.

SUMMARY

This examination of employment in the commodity-producing industries has shown that, with respect to the timing of turning points and durations of cycles and intracycle phases, the behavior of employment in this group of industries was very similar to that in the rest of the nation. The only significant difference in timing was that the Southeast lagged behind the nation by 5.0 months at the peak of Cycle III.

It appears that this difference in timing during Cycle III was created by contract construction employment; for Southeastern contract construction employment lagged behind the corresponding series in the United States by 7.0 months at the peak of Cycle III, and there was no significant difference in turning points of mining and manufacturing employment in the Southeast relative to the United States during this cycle.

With respect to all four cycles, contract construction employment also revealed more (and longer) differences in timing between the Southeast and the United States than did the other two component series. Contract construction employment in the Southeast, in fact, tended to turn more or less independently of the corresponding series in the United States; furthermore, it appeared to turn somewhat independently of mining and manufacturing employment. Significant differences in turning points between the Southeast and the nation for mining and manufacturing employment were confined to only one cycle for each series.[3]

[3] There were three significant differences in timing of the component series (one for each series) which did not show up in the parent sector, nor were they offset. This was apparently due to differences in the relative rates of change of the Southeastern component series as compared to the relative rates of change of the United States com-

For employment in the Southeastern commodity-producing sector, the expansion phase was significantly longer and the contraction phase significantly shorter than for the corresponding series in the United States during Cycle III. And during Cycle IV the expansion phase and the full cycle were significantly longer in the Southeast. The average durations of expansion and contraction and the full-cycle durations (including that of Cycles III and IV), however, were quite similar for the Southeast and the United States.

As in the case of timing, contract construction employment appears to have accounted for the differences during Cycle III. Whereas the expansion and contraction phases of Cycle III of mining and manufacturing were very similar for the Southeast and the United States, Southeastern contract construction employment revealed a longer expansion phase and a shorter contraction phase than did contract construction in the United States. The differences noted for Cycle IV were created by two insignificant differences in timing of the commodity-producing sectors.

Southeastern contract construction employment also seems to have played another interesting role with respect to duration. In this instance it seems to have prevented rather than caused a difference in the behavior of the Southeastern parent series compared with the national parent series. The average expansion phase was 2.7 months longer and the average contraction phase was significantly shorter for Southeastern manufacturing employment than for national manufacturing employment. For Southeastern contract construction, however, the average expansion phase was shorter and the average contraction phase longer than in the counterpart series for the United States. There were no significant differences for mining employment. Thus, contract construc-

---

ponent series. The differences in question occurred in mining employment at the terminal trough of Cycle IV, in contract construction employment at the terminal trough of Cycle II, and in manufacturing employment at the terminal trough of Cycle I.

tion employment prevented the differences between average expansion and average contraction of manufacturing employment in the Southeast compared with the United States from creating a difference between the intracycle durations of the corresponding parent sectors.

While commodity-producing employment in the Southeast revealed a slightly larger average expansion amplitude than did the corresponding series in the United States, the average contraction and the average full-cycle amplitudes were smaller. Thus, on balance, this sector was somewhat more stable in the Southeast. The greater stability of commodity-producing employment in the Southeast was clearly created in manufacturing employment. Mining and contract construction employment were more unstable, overall, in the Southeast than in the nation. But in spite of the greater weight and the instability of these two series in the Southeast, the stability of manufacturing employment in the Southeast, compared with manufacturing employment in the United States as a whole, created a somewhat more stable commodity-producing sector in the Southeast.

The timing of turning points of manufacturing employment in the Southeast was very similar to the turning points of the corresponding series in the United States. The only significant difference occurred during Cycle I and cannot be further investigated because of deficiencies in the available data.[4] These differences did not show up in the parent sector. One, a 5.0 month lag at the peak, was offset by a lead of 7.0 months by Southeast contract construction employment. The other, a 4.0 month lead at the terminal trough, did not create any significant difference in the parent sectors.

Both durable-goods manufacturing employment and

[4] The component employment series of manufacturing employment (durable-goods and nondurable-goods) did not go back far enough to include Cycle I and covered only the contraction phase of Cycle II. Consequently, it is not possible to determine to which of these series the difference in timing can be attributed.

nondurable-goods manufacturing employment in the Southeast turned considerably later than their respective national counterparts at the peak of Cycle III. These differences in timing were not reflected in the parent series. There were, however, deficiencies in the employment data for the Southeastern durable-goods and nondurable-goods series. These series did not include data for two of the Southeastern states; South Carolina and West Virginia. Furthermore, the differences detected in timing may have been exaggerated, for dating the peaks of Cycle III in the United States series was rendered more difficult by the general trend of these series. Further, the date selected for the peak of United States nondurable-goods employment of Cycle III did not correspond closely to the general reference-cycle date, whereas the peak selected for Southeastern nondurable-goods employment did correspond closely to the general reference-cycle date. This was not, however, true of the peak of Cycle III in United States durable-goods employment compared with the peak of the general reference cycle.

A related series, average weekly hours of production workers in manufacturing, was examined in connection with manufacturing employment. There were no significant differences between turning points of average weekly hours in the Southeast and the United States.

The only significant differences between cycle and intra-cycle durations of manufacturing employment in the Southeast and the United States occurred during Cycles I and II. Since the two component series and the related series did not cover these two cycles completely, it was not possible to determine which of these series accounted for the differences.

The really important differential cyclical behavior of manufacturing employment in the Southeast, compared with that of the nation, seemed to be in the size of amplitudes. The average expansion amplitude of manufacturing employment was the same for the Southeast and the United States. But the average contraction amplitudes and the average full-cycle amplitudes were smaller for the Southeast than for the

United States, which may be attributed to the greater weight of nondurable-goods manufacturing in the Southeast.

Unfortunately, the two component series do not include data for South Carolina and West Virginia nor for two of the cycles. If only the last two cycles of manufacturing employment are considered, the average expansion amplitude would be larger for the Southeast than for the United States. The average contraction and full-cycle amplitudes would, however, still be smaller for the Southeast than for the United States. The greater expansion and the smaller contraction amplitudes for the Southeast can be attributed to both durable-goods and nondurable-goods manufacturing employment. However, the smaller full-cycle amplitude in the Southeast is contrary to the behavior of the two component series.

Differences between amplitudes of average weekly hours of production workers in manufacturing in the Southeast and the United States were too small to be considered with respect to the differential behavior noted for the Southeastern manufacturing sector.

5

SERVICES INDUSTRIES EMPLOYMENT

THE TOTAL services sector of nonagricultural industries includes transportation and public utilities, wholesale and retail trade, finance (including insurance and real estate), services and miscellaneous, and government (federal, state, and local). Employment in the service industries is larger than employment in commodity-producing industries; furthermore, employment in these industries has been growing faster in importance, both relatively and absolutely,[1] than employment in the commodity-producing industries.

[1] See Appendix A for sources, description, and evaluation of data used in this chapter.

TOTAL SERVICES SECTOR

In 1945, employment in the nationwide services industries represented 56.7 percent of total nonagricultural employment; by 1961 the proportion had increased to 63.6 percent. In absolute numbers the increase was from 22.9 million in 1945 to 34.4 million in 1961.

Total services employment in the Southeastern region of the United States was 3.6 million in 1945 and represented 57.1 percent of this region's total nonagricultural employment. In 1961 services employment in this region had increased to 6.0 million, representing 63.2 percent of nonagricultural employment. The Southeast has also increased its share of nationwide employment in this sector; the increase was from 15.8 percent in 1945 to 17.6 percent in 1961.

Timing

From the comparison of timing in Table 5-1 one can see that there was no significant difference in timing between the Southeast and the United States. In fact, the average lead or lag was zero at peaks and troughs.

The services sector employment series, of the Southeast and the United States, turned significantly later than total nonagricultural employment and total employment in the commodity-producing sector at the peaks of all four cycles. The only significant differences at the troughs, however, occurred in Cycle II when total services employment led total nonagricultural employment by 3.0 months and led total employment in commodity-producing industries by 5.0 months.

The timing of all three series, however, was virtually the same as that of their respective counterparts in the United States.

Durations

The average durations of cycles and intracycle phases of this series in the Southeast were virtually the same as for the

TABLE 5-1
TURNING POINTS, DURATIONS, AND AMPLITUDES OF CYCLES IN EMPLOYMENT IN SERVICES, UNITED STATES AND SOUTHEAST

Cycle	Turning points			S.E. lead (—) or lag (+) (months)		Durations (months)			Amplitudes		
	Init. Trough	Peak	Term. Trough	Peak	Trough	Expan.	Contr.	Full Cycle	Expan.	Contr.	Full Cycle
Cycle I											
U.S.	9/45	12/48	11/49	—1.0	0.0	39.0	11.0	50.0	+13.7	—0.8	14.5
S.E.	10/45	11/48	11/49			37.0	12.0	49.0	+14.0	—0.6	14.6
Cycle II											
U.S.	11/49	10/53	3/54	0.0	0.0	47.0	5.0	52.0	+11.1	—0.3	11.4
S.E.	11/49	10/53	3/54			47.0	5.0	52.0	+17.2	—0.1	17.3
Cycle III											
U.S.	3/54	8/57	4/58	+1.0	+2.0	41.0	8.0	49.0	+ 9.4	—1.2	10.6
S.E.	3/54	9/57	6/58			42.0	9.0	51.0	+12.1	—0.2	12.3
Cycle IV											
U.S.	4/58	11/60	4/61	0.0	—2.0	31.0	5.0	36.0	+ 6.6	—0.1	6.7
S.E.	6/58	11/60	2/61			29.0	3.0	32.0	+ 7.5	—0.1	7.6
Average[a]											
U.S.				0.0	0.0	39.5	7.3	46.8	+10.2	—0.6	10.8
S.E.						38.8	7.3	46.0	+12.7	—0.3	13.0

[a] Each column averaged separately.
Source: See Appendix A.

corresponding series in the United States. An examination of the individual cycles indicates that the only significant difference occurred in Cycle IV when the full-cycle duration was 4.0 months shorter in the Southeast than in the nation as a whole.

Comparison of this series in the Southeast with the total nonagricultural and commodity-producing series in the Southeast shows that the full-cycle duration was roughly the same for all three. However, the expansion phase of employment in the services sector was significantly longer and the contraction phase was significantly shorter than for the corresponding phases in the other two series.

Relative to their respective counterparts for the United States, total nonagricultural employment and the two component employment series in the Southeast behaved very similarly with respect to duration.

Amplitudes

The average amplitudes were larger for the Southeast than for the United States during the full cycle and the expansion phase. However, the average amplitude during the contraction phase was smaller for the Southeast than for the United States.

The individual full-cycle amplitudes were greater for the Southeast than for the United States during all four cycles. The same was true for expansion amplitudes. Contraction amplitudes, on the other hand, were smaller for the Southeast during three cycles and the same as for the United States during the other cycle.

All amplitudes for the services sector were considerably smaller than those for total nonagricultural employment and employment in commodity-producing industries, an indication that employment in services industries was less sensitive to cyclical forces than either employment in the commodity-producing sector or total nonagricultural employment. This holds true for the Southeast and for the United States.

But the behavior of amplitudes for the Southeast relative

to those of the United States indicates that the Southeast services sector was slightly more sensitive to cyclical fluctuations than either the Southeast commodity-producing sector or Southeast total nonagricultural employment.

TRANSPORTATION AND PUBLIC UTILITIES

Employment in transportation and public utilities (hereafter referred to as "transportation") remained virtually constant over the postwar years, a pattern true in the United States and in the Southeast. As a percentage of total employment in the services sector, employment in transportation declined substantially for both the nation as a whole and the Southeastern states.

In 1945, 3.9 million workers were employed in transportation industries throughout the nation and the number was unchanged by 1961, although employment was slightly above 4.0 million on several occasions during this period. In 1945 employment in these industries represented 17.1 percent of total services employment in the United States. But by 1961 transportation accounted for only 11.4 percent of total services employment.

In the Southeast, employment in transportation was 626,000 in 1945 and 670,000 in 1961. These workers represented 17.4 percent of employment in the Southeastern services sector in 1945 and 11.1 percent in 1961. The Southeastern states increased their share of nationwide transportation employment over the postwar period from 16.0 percent in 1945 to 17.1 percent in 1961.

Timing

The comparison of turning points (Table 5-2) of transportation employment for the Southeast and the United States shows that this series in the Southeast lagged behind the corresponding series in the United States at all four peaks, although only two of the lags were significant.

Employment in Southeastern transportation did not

conform to its counterpart in the nation quite as well as employment in the parent Southeastern services sector conformed to its national counterpart, but the differences were negligible.

Comparison of transportation employment in the Southeastern states with the parent sector in the Southeast indicates that the former led the latter at all four peaks. However, only one of these leads was significant and that was a 6.0 month lead in Cycle IV. At the troughs, transportation in the Southeast lagged behind the parent sector in three of the four cycles, but again only one was a significant lag and this lag also occurred in Cycle IV, when transportation employment turned 3.0 months later than total services employment. Transportation employment for the United States also led the parent sector in the United States at peaks and lagged at troughs. These differences were more pronounced, in fact, for the United States than for the Southeast.

Durations

The average duration of full cycles in transportation employment was virtually the same for the Southeast and the United States. Significant differences did occur, however, in the average durations of the expansion and the contraction phases for the Southeast and the United States. The expansion phase was an average of 3.5 months longer in the Southeast than in the nation as a whole; the contraction phase, on the other hand, was an average of 3.8 months shorter in the Southeast than in the United States.

Examination of the individual cycles reveals that on no occasion was there a significant difference in full-cycle durations between the Southeast and the United States. The expansion phase was longer in the Southeast than in the United States during all cycles; it was significantly longer during Cycles II-IV. During these three cycles the expansion phases were 4.0 months, 6.0 months, and 3.0 months (respectively) longer in the Southeast than in the nation.

TABLE 5-2

Turning Points, Durations, and Amplitudes of Cycles in Transportation and Public Utilities Employment, United States and Southeast

Cycle	Turning points			S.E. lead (−) or lag (+) (months)		Durations (months)			Amplitudes		
	Init. Trough	Peak	Term. Trough	Peak	Trough	Expan.	Contr.	Full Cycle	Expan.	Contr.	Full Cycle
Cycle I											
U.S.	9/45	7/48	10/49			34.0	15.0	49.0	+ 7.3	−7.4	14.7
S.E.	10/45	9/48	10/49	+2.0	0.0	35.0	13.0	48.0	+10.0	−9.3	19.3
Cycle II											
U.S.	10/49	5/53	11/54			43.0	18.0	61.0	+ 9.9	−6.4	16.3
S.E.	10/49	9/53	9/54	+4.0	−2.0	47.0	12.0	59.0	+11.9	−5.1	17.0
Cycle III											
U.S.	11/54	4/57	9/58			29.0	17.0	46.0	+ 5.6	−8.3	13.9
S.E.	9/54	8/57	7/58	+4.0	−2.0	35.0	11.0	46.0	+ 7.8	−6.0	13.8
Cycle IV											
U.S.	9/55	4/60	5/61			19.0	13.0	32.0	+ 2.2	−3.5	5.7
S.E.	7/58	5/60	5/61	+1.0	0.0	22.0	12.0	34.0	+ 2.4	−3.6	6.0
Average[a]											
U.S.						31.3	15.8	47.0	+ 6.3	−6.4	12.7
S.E.				+2.8	−1.0	34.8	12.0	46.8	+ 8.0	−6.0	14.0

[a] Each column averaged separately.
Source: See Appendix A.

On the other hand, the contraction phase was shorter in the Southeast than in the nation as a whole during all cycles. The difference was 6.0 months during Cycles II and III, but the other two differences were insignificant.

Durations of the intracycle phases of Southeastern transportation and of United States transportation employment show greater disparity than do the parent series for the Southeast and the United States.

The duration of the expansion phase of transportation employment in the Southeast and the United States tended to be shorter than the expansion phase of employment in the services sector while the duration of the contraction phases was longer. The full-cycle durations of transportation employment in the Southeast and the United States, however, were virtually the same as for their respective parent sectors.

Amplitudes

The average full-cycle amplitude of transportation employment was larger for the Southeast than for the United States. Full-cycle amplitudes were also larger for the Southeast during all individual cycles except Cycle III, which was virtually the same as the United States series.

The average expansion amplitude was also larger for the Southeast than for the nation as a whole. The individual Southeastern cycles were also larger in expansion amplitude.

The average contraction amplitude was slightly smaller for the Southeast than for the United States. However, no set pattern of relative contraction amplitudes emerged for this series. During Cycles I and IV the contraction amplitudes were larger for the Southeast than for the nation as a whole (although the difference between contraction amplitudes in Cycle IV was so small it could have been due to rounding). During Cycles II and III the contraction amplitudes were smaller for the Southeast than for the United States.

Relative to their respective national counterparts, employment in Southeastern transportation and employment in the Southeastern services sector behaved similarly with regard to cyclical fluctuations. In general, however, both series showed larger expansion and full-cycle amplitudes and smaller contraction amplitudes than they did for the United States.

Comparison of full-cycle amplitudes of transportation employment in the Southeast with those of Southeastern employment in the services sector reveals that the fluctuations were slightly larger for the transportation series. The fluctuation was considerably larger for transportation employment during the contraction phase, but during expansion it was less for transportation than for the parent series. The relationship between full-cycle and intracycle amplitudes of transportation employment and employment in the services sector was the same for the United States as for the Southeast.

WHOLESALE AND RETAIL TRADE

In contrast to transportation employment, employment in wholesale and retail trade (hereafter referred to simply as "trade") in the United States and in the Southeast, increased absolutely and as a percentage of total employment in the services sector.

There were 7.3 million workers in nationwide trade establishments in 1945 and 11.4 million workers in these establishments in 1961, representing 31.9 percent of total national employment in the services sector in 1945 and 33.1 percent in 1961.

In the Southeastern states, 1.1 million employees were employed in trade industries in 1945 and 2.0 million in 1961. Employment in Southeastern trade establishments represented 31.7 percent of total Southeastern services employment in 1945 and 33.7 percent in 1961. The Southeast also increased its share of the nation's trade employment during the period 1945-1961. In 1945 the Southeast had 15.6 percent of total United States trade employment; in 1961, Southeastern trade employment represented 17.9 percent of the national total.

Timing

Southeastern trade employment did not show any tendency to lead or lag behind its counterpart in the nation as a whole (Table 5-3). The only significant difference in turning points between the Southeast and the United States occurred during Cycle I, when the Southeast led the nation by 4.0 months at the trough.

Turning points of Southeast trade employment conformed more closely to the corresponding series in the United States than transportation employment in the Southeast corresponded to its national counterpart. Both of these component series in the Southeast revealed more significant differences in timing than the parent series, when compared with their respective counterparts in the nation.

Trade employment in the Southeast led transportation employment in the Southeast at each of the four terminal troughs, but only two leads were significant. Trade employment also led transportation employment by 6.0 months at the initial trough of Cycle I. Although Southeastern trade employment tended to lead Southeastern transportation employment at troughs, this tendency did not prevail with respect to peaks.

The lead or lag relationship between Southeastern trade employment and total employment in the Southeastern services sector did not exhibit a clear pattern. However, some significant differences in timing for the two series were observed. Trade employment in the Southeast led the parent sector by 5.0 months at the peak of Cycle III and by 7.0 months at the peak of Cycle IV. At troughs, the component series led 6.0 months at the initial trough of Cycle I and 8.0 months at the terminal trough of this cycle. And in Cycle II, trade employment lagged behind the parent series by 3.0 months at the terminal trough. The same general

TABLE 5-3
Turning Points, Durations, and Amplitudes of Cycles in Trade Employment,
United States and Southeast

Cycle	Turning points			S.E. lead (−) or lag (+) (months)		Durations (months)			Amplitudes		
	Init. Trough	Peak	Term. Trough	Peak	Trough	Expan.	Contr.	Full Cycle	Expan.	Contr.	Full Cycle
Cycle I											
U.S.	4/45	11/48	7/49			43.0	8.0	51.0	+24.8	−1.3	26.1
S.E.	4/45	10/48	3/49	−1.0	−4.0	42.0	5.0	47.0	+30.2	−0.7	30.9
Cycle II											
U.S.	7/49	10/53	6/54			51.0	8.0	59.0	+10.7	−0.7	11.4
S.E.	3/49	9/53	6/54	−1.0	0.0	54.0	9.0	63.0	+15.4	−1.2	16.6
Cycle III											
U.S.	6/54	4/57	4/58			34.0	12.0	46.0	+6.4	−2.1	8.5
S.E.	6/54	4/57	4/58	0.0	0.0	34.0	12.0	46.0	+10.2	−1.8	12.0
Cycle IV											
U.S.	4/58	4/60	4/61			24.0	12.0	36.0	+6.4	−1.0	7.4
S.E.	4/58	4/60	4/61	0.0	0.0	24.0	12.0	36.0	+6.5	−0.4	6.9
Average[a]											
U.S.						38.0	10.0	48.0	+12.1	−1.3	13.4
S.E.				−0.5	−1.0	38.5	9.5	48.0	+15.6	−1.0	16.6

[a] Each column averaged separately.
Source: See Appendix A.

pattern of leads and lags noted for the Southeast, with respect to the comparison of trade employment with transportation and services employment, also applied to these series in the United States.

Durations

The average durations of the full cycle, the expansion phase, and the contraction phase of this series were virtually the same for the Southeast and the United States. Significant differences occurred during Cycles I and II. The contraction phase of Cycle I was 3.0 months shorter for the Southeast than for the United States and the full cycle was 4.0 months shorter; during Cycle II the expansion phase was 3.0 months longer and the full cycle was 4.0 months longer for the Southeast than for the United States.

Durations of cycles and intracycle phases of employment in Southeastern trade establishments conformed more closely to the United States series than did durations of cycles and intracycle phases of transportation employment. However, neither of the component series in the Southeast conformed as well as the parent sector in the Southeast when compared to their corresponding series in the nation.

Overall, there was little difference between the average full-cycle durations of trade employment in the Southeast and transportation employment in the Southeast. The clearest pattern, with respect to the relative durations of cycles and cycle phases in these two series, was during the expansion phases. The expansion phase was longer for Southeastern trade employment during three of the four cycles and its average duration of expansion was 3.7 months longer than the average expansion duration of transportation employment. The average duration of contraction was 2.5 months shorter for Southeastern trade employment than for Southeastern transportation employment.

In the United States as a whole, the average duration of expansion was 6.7 months longer for trade employment than for transportation employment and the average duration of contraction was 5.8 months shorter for trade employment than for transportation employment. The average length of the full cycle was roughly the same for both series in the United States.

Although there was no significant difference between trade employment in the Southeast and the United States, when compared with their respective parent sectors, with regard to average durations of cycles and intracycle phases, the contraction phase was generally longer for trade employment than for employment in the services sector.

Amplitudes

Average amplitudes for the full cycle and the expansion phase were larger for the Southeast than for the United States, while the average amplitude of contraction was smaller.

During each cycle the expansion amplitude was larger, and the contraction amplitude was smaller for the Southeast than for the United States. In three of the four cycles the full-cycle amplitude was larger for the Southeast than for the United States. Cycle IV was the exception, with the full-cycle amplitude being slightly smaller than for the United States.

The cyclical fluctuations of trade employment in the Southeast relative to the fluctuations of the corresponding series in the nation as a whole followed the same pattern as transportation and total services employment. That is, the three series for the Southeast had larger amplitudes of expansion and the full cycle and smaller amplitudes of contraction than their respective counterparts in the United States.

The magnitude of the fluctuations during the full cycle and the expansion phase was greater for trade employment in the Southeast than for either Southeastern transportation employment or Southeastern services employment. The magnitude of the average contraction amplitude was slightly larger for the Southeastern trade employment than for the services sector; but it was considerably smaller than the average contraction amplitude for transportation employment. This was also true of the amplitudes of these series for the United States as a whole.

FINANCE

Finance employment, including insurance and real estate, increased consistently from 1945 to 1961 in the United States and in the Southeast. Employment in finance industries also increased as a proportion of total services employment.

In the United States, 1.5 million workers were employed in finance establishments in 1945 and this figure had increased to 2.7 million by 1961. As percentages of total United States services employment, these workers represented 6.5 percent and 8.0 percent for the years 1945 and 1961, respectively.

The increase was greater for the Southeast than for the nation as a whole. Employment in Southeastern finance industries increased from 144,000 employees to 425,000 in 1961. In absolute numbers the increase was almost threefold. Southeastern finance employment was 4.0 percent of Southeastern services employment in 1945; it was 7.9 percent in 1961. The Southeast also increased its share of the nation's finance employment over the postwar years from 9.6 percent in 1945 to 15.4 percent in 1961.

Timing

Finance employment in the Southeast showed no tendency to lead the corresponding series in the nation at the peaks (Table 5-4). There was some tendency, however, for this series in the Southeast to lead its counterpart in the United States at the troughs. The average lead at troughs was 2.5 months, not quite a significant difference. But inspection of the separate cycles indicates that the Southeast led the nation at the troughs of each cycle. Only two of these leads were significant. During Cycle II the Southeast led by 4.0 months and during Cycle III the Southeast led the nation by 3.0 months. There were also two significant differences in turning points at the peaks, although the average lead or lag was zero. At the peak of Cycles I and II the Southeast lagged behind the nation by 4.0 months.

Finance employment in the Southeast revealed more divergencies in timing than either Southeastern transportation, trade, or total services employment, when compared with their respective national counterparts.

Southeastern finance employment consistently lagged Southeastern transportation employment at peaks. All of the lags were significant except for a 2.0 month lag at the peak of Cycle I. At the trough, finance employment led the transportation employment series for the Southeast. All of these leads were significant, including a lead at the initial trough of Cycle I.

Finance employment in the Southeast also lagged Southeastern trade employment at each of the four peaks. Again, these lags were significant with the exception of Cycle I. But these two Southeastern employment series turned at approximately the same time at the troughs. Turning points of finance and trade employment in the United States as a whole revealed roughly the same relative behavior as did those of these two series in the Southeast.

Finance employment showed no tendency to lead or lag behind the parent series at peaks or troughs, in the Southeast or the United States.

Durations

The average full-cycle duration of finance employment was virtually the same for the Southeast and the United States. The only significant difference in full-cycle duration of this series in the Southeast from that of the United States was for Cycle I. For this cycle, the full-cycle duration was 3.0 months longer for the Southeast than for the nation as a whole.

The average expansion phase was slightly longer for the

TABLE 5-4
TURNING POINTS, DURATIONS, AND AMPLITUDES OF CYCLES IN FINANCE EMPLOYMENT,
UNITED STATES AND SOUTHEAST

Cycle	Turning points			S.E. lead (−) or lag (+) (months)		Durations (months)			Amplitudes		
	Init. Trough	Peak	Term. Trough	Peak	Trough	Expan.	Contr.	Full Cycle	Expan.	Contr.	Full Cycle
Cycle I											
U.S.	4/45	7/48	7/49	+4.0	−2.0	39.0	12.0	51.0	+21.4	+0.7	20.7
S.E.	5/45	11/48	5/49			42.0	6.0	48.0	+31.6	−1.7	33.3
Cycle II											
U.S.	7/49	4/53	8/54	−4.0	−4.0	57.0	4.0	61.0	+17.8	+1.5	16.3
S.E.	5/49	12/53	4/54			55.0	4.0	59.0	+38.7	+1.3	37.4
Cycle III											
U.S.	8/54	12/57	7/58	0.0	−3.0	40.0	7.0	47.0	+11.0	+0.2	10.8
S.E.	4/54	12/57	4/58			44.0	4.0	48.0	+21.5	+0.6	20.9
Cycle IV											
U.S.	7/58	10/60	3/61	0.0	−1.0	27.0	5.0	32.0	+7.0	+0.9	6.1
S.E.	4/58	10/60	2/61			30.0	4.0	34.0	+12.9	+0.8	12.1
Average[a]											
U.S.				0.0	−2.5	40.8	7.0	47.8	+14.3	+0.8	13.5
S.E.						42.8	4.5	47.3	+26.2	+0.3	25.9

[a] Each column averaged separately.
Source: See Appendix A.

Southeast than for the United States. And from the individual cycles we see that this phase was significantly longer in the Southeast during three of the four cycles. The expansion was longer in the Southeast by 3.0 months in Cycle I, 4.0 months in Cycle III, and 3.0 months in Cycle IV.

Contraction, on the other hand, was slightly shorter for the Southeast than for the United States on the average. During Cycle I contraction was 6.0 months less and during Cycle III 3.0 months less for the Southeast than for the nation.

Overall, the full-cycle durations of Southeastern finance, transportation, and trade employment were about the same. But the average duration of expansion was significantly longer for finance than for either transportation or trade employment, and the average contraction phase was significantly shorter for finance than for either of the other two component series. With respect to cycle and intracycle durations, Southeastern finance employment had roughly the same relationship to the services sector as it did to the series of trade and transportation, a relationship which also held true for the corresponding series in the United States.

Amplitudes

The average amplitudes for the full cycle, the expansion phase, and the contraction phase were larger for the Southeast than for the United States. During the expansion phase and the full cycle, the average amplitudes were considerably larger for the Southeast. The average contraction amplitude was positive for the Southeast and the United States, and both amplitudes were very small.

Examination of the separate cycles reveals that the full-cycle amplitudes were larger for the Southeast than for the nation during all four cycles. This was also true of expansion amplitudes. During contraction the cyclical change was larger for the Southeast during three of the four cycles, but smaller during Cycle III.

Finance employment in the Southeast was substantially

less stable during cyclical movements than Southeastern transportation, trade, or total services employment when compared with their national counterparts.

The magnitude of the amplitudes of finance employment for the Southeast and for the United States was greater than those in transportation, trade, or total services employment during the full cycle and the expansion phase, but contraction amplitudes were smaller.

SERVICES AND MISCELLANEOUS INDUSTRIES

Employment in services and miscellaneous industries has increased steadily in the Southeast and the United States since 1945. Employment in these establishments has also increased as a proportion of total services employment.[2]

In 1945 employment in miscellaneous industries in the United States was 4.2 million, representing 18.5 percent of total United States services employment; there were 7.5 million employees in these industries in 1961, representing 21.9 percent of total services employment.

In the Southeast, miscellaneous employment increased from 576,000 in 1945 to 1.2 million in 1961. Miscellaneous employment in the Southeast represented 16.0 percent of employment in the total Southeastern services sector in 1945 and 19.9 percent in 1961. The Southeast has also increased its share of nationwide miscellaneous employment from 13.6 percent in 1945 to 16.0 percent in 1961.

Timing

Table 5-5 shows that miscellaneous employment in the Southeast led the corresponding series in the United States at three of the four peaks. Only one of these leads, a 3.0

[2] The services and miscellaneous series is primarily a residual classification, including mostly personal services. To avoid confusion between this series and the parent services sector, services and miscellaneous employment will be henceforth referred to as "miscellaneous" employment.

month lead at the peak of Cycle I, was significant. The average lead was only 1.8 months.

At troughs, miscellaneous employment in the Southeast also led its counterpart in the United States on three occasions; two of these were significant. The average lead at troughs was 1.8 months—the same as the average lead at peaks.

Turning points of miscellaneous employment in the Southeast were significantly different from those of its counterpart in the United States on more occasions than was true of the corresponding employment series of transportation, trade, or total services, but not that of finance.

Southeastern miscellaneous employment tended to lead Southeastern employment in transportation, finance, and the services sector at peaks. It led employment in finance and employment in the total services sector more often than it led trade employment. Miscellaneous employment in the Southeast also tended to turn earlier at troughs than either of its companion series or the parent series. Of these series it led transportation employment by the largest margin. The above pattern was generally true of these series in the United States as well as for the Southeast.

Durations

The average cycle and intracycle durations of miscellaneous employment were virtually the same for the United States and the Southeast. One can see from an inspection of the separate cycles that only one significant difference occurred between full-cycle durations of the Southeast and the United States and only one significant difference of expansion durations. The full cycle duration was 3.0 months shorter for the Southeast than for the United States during Cycle III and the expansion phase of Cycle I was 3.0 months shorter for the Southeast than for the United States. Differences of contraction duration between the United States and the Southeast were insignificant.

With respect to the duration of cycles and cycle phases,

TABLE 5-5
TURNING POINTS, DURATIONS, AND AMPLITUDES OF CYCLES IN SERVICES AND MISCELLANEOUS EMPLOYMENT, UNITED STATES AND SOUTHEAST

Cycle	Turning points			S.E. lead (−) or lag (+) (months)		Durations (months)			Amplitudes		
	Init. Trough	Peak	Term. Trough	Peak	Trough	Expan.	Contr.	Full Cycle	Expan.	Contr.	Full Cycle
Cycle I											
U.S.	4/45	9/48	3/49			41.0	6.0	47.0	+22.0	+0.2	21.8
S.E.	4/45	6/48	2/49	−3.0	−1.0	38.0	8.0	46.0	+22.6	+0.2	22.4
Cycle II											
U.S.	3/49	6/53	2/54			51.0	8.0	59.0	+10.9	+1.4	9.5
S.E.	2/49	6/53	2/54	0.0	0.0	52.0	8.0	60.0	+22.2	+1.1	21.1
Cycle III											
U.S.	2/54	9/57	6/58			43.0	9.0	52.0	+13.4	−0.1	13.5
S.E.	2/54	7/57	3/58	−2.0	−3.0	41.0	8.0	49.0	+14.5	+0.1	14.4
Cycle IV											
U.S.	6/58	11/60	5/61			29.0	6.0	35.0	+8.6	+0.2	8.8
S.E.	3/58	9/60	2/61	−2.0	−3.0	30.0	5.0	35.0	+12.3	+0.3	12.0
Average[a]											
U.S.						41.0	7.3	48.3	+13.7	+0.4	13.4
S.E.				−1.8	−1.8	40.3	7.3	47.5	+17.9	+0.4	17.5

[a] Each column averaged separately.
Source: See Appendix A.

Southeastern miscellaneous employment was more similar to the corresponding series in the United States than Southeastern transportation, trade, or finance employment were to their respective national counterparts.

The average lengths of the full cycles and the intracycle phases of miscellaneous employment in the Southeast were also more similar to those of the parent sector than to those of transportation, trade, or finance. There was virtually no difference between the average full-cycle duration of miscellaneous employment in the Southeast and transportation, trade, or finance employment in the Southeast. However, significant differences between expansion and contraction durations of miscellaneous employment in the Southeast and those of transportation employment in the Southeast were observed. The expansion phase of miscellaneous employment was 5.5 months longer than for transportation employment and the contraction phase was 4.7 months longer.

The average durations of the full cycle, the expansion phase, and the contraction phase of miscellaneous employment in the United States revealed about the same relationship to the average durations of the full cycle and intracycle phases of transportation, trade, finance, and the total services sector as noted above for these series in the Southeast.

Amplitudes

A comparison of average amplitudes of miscellaneous employment in the Southeast and the United States shows that cyclical fluctuations were greater for the Southeast than for the United States during the full cycle and the expansion phase. The average fluctuation was the same for both series during contraction.

Examination of the individual cycles reveals that the full-cycle and expansion amplitudes were larger for the Southeast than for the United States during each cycle. And the contraction amplitudes were approximately the same for the Southeast and the United States during each cycle.

The relative behavior of amplitudes of this series for the

United States and the Southeast was not appreciably different from the parent series or the transportation, trade, and finance series.

However, the magnitude of the full-cycle and expansion fluctuations of miscellaneous employment in the Southeast and the United States was larger than for transportation, trade, or the services sector, but smaller than for finance. The size of the contraction amplitude of miscellaneous employment in the Southeast and the United States, on the other hand, was smaller than for any of the four series mentioned above.

GOVERNMENT

Government employment, including federal, state, and local government, in the Southeast and the United States declined from 1945 to its lowest point of the postwar period in 1947. Since 1947, government employment has been increasing steadily. Because of the decline immediately following the war, it appeared more appropriate to measure the postwar changes in employment from 1947 rather than 1945.

Total government employment throughout the nation increased from 5.5 million in 1947 to 8.8 million in 1961. Government workers represented 21.6 percent of total services employment in 1947 and 25.7 in 1961.

In the Southeast, government employment was 993,000 in 1947 and 1.7 million in 1961. As a percentage of total services employment in the Southeast, these employees represented 25.2 percent in 1947 and 28.3 percent in 1961. The proportion of nationwide government employment in the Southeast increased slightly over this period. In 1947, government employment in the Southeastern states amounted to 18.1 percent of government employment in the United States; in 1961, the Southeastern share was 19.3 percent.

Timing

Turning points of government employment were virtually the same for the Southeast and the United States.

Differences in timing of the two corresponding series were few and very small (Table 5-6). Relative to its corresponding series in the United States, government employment in the Southeast was more congruous than any of the component series of the services sector and was about the same as the parent sector.

The actual turning points of government employment in the Southeast and in the United States were quite different from those of the other component series and the parent series in the Southeast and the United States. Government employment lagged behind all of the other services series by a considerable amount at all turning points of Cycle I. The longest lag was at the initial trough of this cycle; at this turning point government employment turned approximately two years later than the other employment series of this sector. During Cycle II, the peak and terminal trough occurred much earlier than those of the other services series. In Cycle III, the peak was in the general vicinity of the peak of the other services series but the trough was considerably earlier. And Cycle IV followed the same pattern as Cycle III. Thus, there was no set behavior of this series in relation to its companion series or to its parent series, for the Southeast or for the United States.

Durations

The average durations of the full cycles and the intracycle phases were very similar for the Southeast and the United States; two significant differences, however, in full-cycle durations did emerge: Cycle II was 3.0 months shorter and Cycle III was 4.0 months longer in the Southeast than in the United States.

Government employment in the Southeast was more similar to its national counterpart than any of the companion series were to their respective national counterparts, with respect to durations of cycles and cycle phases. It was very similar to the parent series in this respect.

Cycles and intracycles phases tended to be much shorter

TABLE 5-6
TURNING POINTS, DURATIONS, AND AMPLITUDES OF CYCLES IN GOVERNMENT EMPLOYMENT, UNITED STATES AND SOUTHEAST

Cycle	Turning points			S.E. lead (—) or lag (+) (months)		Durations (months)			Amplitudes		
	Init. Trough	Peak	Term. Trough	Peak	Trough	Expan.	Contr.	Full Cycle	Expan.	Contr.	Full Cycle
Cycle I											
U.S.	8/47	9/49	2/50			25.0	5.0	30.0	+ 7.7	+0.1	7.6
S.E.	9/47	9/49	3/50	0.0	+1.0	24.0	6.0	30.0	+ 8.8	+0.6	8.2
Cycle II											
U.S.	2/50	12/52	7/53			34.0	7.0	41.0	+13.0	−1.7	14.7
S.E.	3/50	12/52	5/53	0.0	−2.0	33.0	5.0	38.0	+17.6	−1.3	18.9
Cycle III											
U.S.	7/53	7/57	10/57			48.0	3.0	51.0	+14.5	+0.4	14.1
S.E.	5/53	7/57	12/57	0.0	+2.0	50.0	5.0	55.0	+15.9	+1.2	14.7
Cycle IV											
U.S.	10/57	3/60	7/60			29.0	4.0	33.0	+ 9.3	+0.1	9.2
S.E.	12/57	4/60	7/60	+1.0	0.0	28.0	3.0	31.0	+ 7.2	+0.5	6.7
Average[a]											
U.S.						34.0	4.8	38.8	+11.1	−0.3	11.4
S.E.				+0.3	+0.3	33.8	4.8	38.5	+12.4	+0.3	12.1

[a] Each column averaged separately.
Source: See Appendix A.

for Southeastern (and national) government employment than for the total services sectors or the other components of the services sector.

Amplitudes

The average amplitudes of the full cycle and the expansion phase were larger for the Southeast than for the United States, and the average contraction amplitude was smaller for the Southeast than for the United States. For the separate cycles, the amplitudes of expansion and the full cycle were also generally larger for the Southeast; Cycle IV was an exception in both cases. On the other hand, contraction amplitudes were smaller for the Southeast during each of the four cycles.

The relative behavior of this series in the Southeast, compared with the national series, followed the relative behavior of all the other services series, except finance, with respect to amplitudes. It will be recalled that the contraction amplitude of finance was slightly larger for the Southeast than for the United States.

Full-cycle amplitudes of government employment in the Southeast tended to be smaller, on the average, than full-cycle amplitudes of any of the other services employment series. The expansion and contraction amplitudes also tended to be smaller for this series. The expansion amplitude, however, was larger than that of transportation employment, and the contraction amplitude approximately the same as those of finance and miscellaneous employment.

The pattern was not quite the same for the United States, for the average full-cycle amplitude of government employment for the United States was slightly larger than the average full-cycle amplitude of total services employment, but smaller than any of the other component series. The average expansion amplitude of government employment for the United States was larger than the average expansion amplitude of total services employment or transportation employment, but smaller than the average expansion amplitude of trade, finance, or miscellaneous employment in the United States. The average contraction amplitude of government employment was larger than the average contraction amplitudes of finance or miscellaneous employment, but smaller than the average contraction amplitudes of total services employment, transportation employment, or trade employment.

SUMMARY

The following generalizations perhaps can be validly drawn from the preceding analysis of the five disaggregated employment series (transportation, trade, finance, miscellaneous, and government industries) comprising the services sector.

The basic difference between the cyclical behavior of total services employment in the Southeast and the United States was found to be in the size of amplitudes. Amplitudes for this series were larger for the Southeast than for the United States during the expansion phase and the full cycle but smaller for the Southeast than for the United States during the contraction phase.

None of the five component series in the Southeast showed a strong tendency to lead or lag the corresponding series in the United States. The closest conformity in timing between the Southeast and the United States was found in the government employment series, and the least conformity was found in the finance employment series.

Comparison of timing of all the component series of the services sector in the Southeast revealed that government employment did not conform at all with the other component Southeastern series or the parent Southeastern series. Of the other four component Southeastern series, finance showed some indication of lagging behind transportation, trade, and miscellaneous employment at the peaks. The differences in the timing of turning points of cycles in the five component series in the Southeast compared with the timing of their respective counterparts in the nation were small.

The full-cycle durations were virtually the same for transportation, trade, finance, and miscellaneous employment in the Southeast. The full-cycle durations for government employment, however, were considerably shorter than those of the other Southeastern components.

In the United States and the Southeast, the average duration of expansion was considerably shorter for government and transportation employment than for trade, finance, or miscellaneous employment. The average contraction duration was shortest in government and finance and longest in transportation employment.

Compared with their respective national counterparts, only the transportation employment series revealed significant differences in average durations of the intracycle phases. For this series, the average expansion phase was longer and the average contraction phase shorter in the Southeast than in the United States. Although the differences were insignificant, the other series were also characterized by longer expansion and shorter contractions in the Southeast. There were no significant differences in average full-cycle durations in the Southeast and the United States for any of these series.

The differences between cycle and intracycle phase durations of the five component series in the Southeast compared with their respective counterparts for the United States were not large enough to have had any appreciable effect on the differential cyclical behavior discussed for the parent sector.

All of the five component series in the Southeast revealed larger amplitudes for the full cycle and the expansion phase than their respective counterparts in the United States. Most of the series revealed smaller amplitudes for the Southeast than for the United States during contraction. Thus, the differential cyclical behavior of the two (Southeast and United States) parent services series stems from similar differences in the cyclical behavior of the five component series in the Southeast compared with their respective counterparts for the nation. Finance and miscellaneous employment appear to have contributed more toward the instability of the parent sector in both areas during contraction periods, while transportation, trade, and government employment have tended to stabilize the parent sector in both areas during contraction periods. All five component series also contributed in both areas to the instability of services employment during the expansion phase and the full cycle. As noted, the five Southeastern components were less stable than their respective United States counterparts, thus occasioning differential cyclical behavior in their parent series.

6

EFFECT OF INDUSTRY-MIX

$\mathcal{I}$NCOME AND employment for the Southeast have been compared with their national counterparts in an effort to isolate any peculiar cyclical characteristics of the Southeast region. These comparisons were made without making allowance for the different industrial compositions of the areas. Indeed, interareal differences of industry-mix were emphasized in drawing conclusions concerning the differential cyclical behavior of the Southeast. And, to be sure, interareal differences in cyclical behavior are more meaningful when determined from comparison of actual rather than hypothetical data. But the preceding analyses leave an interesting question unanswered: What would be the relative cyclical behavior of Southeastern income and employment if the region had the same industry-mix as the United States?

Measuring the effect of industry-mix on the cyclical behavior of the Southeast necessitates adjustment of industrial composition in the Southeast so that it conforms, hypothetically, to that of the United States as a whole. This "standardization" of a region's industry-mix is a statistical technique which has been used recently in the area of regional economics[1] and, in at least one study, a similar technique has been applied specifically to the study of regional cycles.[2] The following is a brief description of the specific procedure used in adjusting the industry-mix of aggregate series for the Southeast.

Initially, each component of an aggregate series in the Southeast was converted to percent relatives using the first month of the series as the base period. In reality it would have made little difference which period was chosen as a base provided the same period was used for each component series. Once the component series were converted to simple percent relatives each component series was then assigned a weight equal to the relative weight of its national counterpart in the national aggregate series. A sum of the weighted components for the Southeast was then used to represent the aggregate series.[3] This aggregate series is of course a

[1] See Edgar S. Dunn, Jr., *Recent Southern Economic Development as Revealed by the Changing Structure of Employment* (Gainsville, Fla.: University of Florida Press, 1962); Harvey S. Perloff and others, *Regions, Resources and Economic Growth* (Baltimore: Johns Hopkins Press, 1960); and Victor H. Fuchs, *Changes in the Location of Manufacturing in the United States Since 1929* (New Haven: Yale University Press, 1962).

[2] See George H. Borts, "Regional Cycles of Manufacturing Employment in the United States, 1914-1953," *Journal of the American Statistical Association*, LV (March 1960), 151-211.

[3] The result is a weighted index which represents the aggregate series. Cyclical measures used in this study are the same whether determined from an index or from the actual values. Thus the weighted

hypothetical series indicating what the aggregate Southeastern series would have been if its industrial composition had been the same as its national counterpart. These hypothetical series for the Southeast were then examined for cyclical movements in the same manner as explained in Chapter I.

Certain limitations to the extent that this technique could be applied exist. Unfortunately, because of limited availability of monthly data for detailed industrial classifications, only four aggregate Southeastern employment series could be adjusted for industrial composition; they were nonagricultural, commodity-producing, services, and manufacturing industries. Their respective components are presented in the appropriate sections below. Available data permitted analysis of all four complete cycles for the first three series mentioned above. However, manufacturing employment could be examined for only two complete cycles; and this series was further limited to only ten of the twelve Southeastern states due to the absence of data for durable-goods and nondurable-goods industries for two states. In addition to these limitations, the statistical technique itself does not allow for any changes in the industrial composition of the areas over the period covered. There are indications that such changes have occurred. It should also be noted that many of the component series were themselves highly aggregative.

Even with these limitations in mind it seemed worthwhile to reexamine these four aggregate series; the results, though not conclusive, should add to the understanding of the relative cyclical behavior of the Southeast region. Quantitative cyclical measures of these four Southeastern employment series adjusted for composition are compared with their unadjusted counterparts in the Southeast and with the corresponding series in the country as a whole.

---

index was used to eliminate a further unnecessary step—that of converting indexes into the actual units of measure.

NONAGRICULTURAL EMPLOYMENT

There were eight components of nonagricultural employment —mining, contract construction, manufacturing, transportation and public utilities, wholesale and retail trade, finance (including real estate and insurance), miscellaneous services, and government (state, local, and federal). Each of these components was assigned a weight equal to its relative weight for the country as a whole—as described above—and the hypothetical nonagricultural series was thus derived for the Southeast region. The quantitative cyclical characteristics of this series are presented in Table 6-1. Also presented in this table, for purposes of comparison, are the cyclical data for United States nonagricultural employment and unadjusted Southeastern nonagricultural employment. These figures are the same as those previously presented in Table 3-2.

Timing and Durations

The adjustment for industry-mix of Southeastern nonagricultural employment altered only two turning points from those previously designated for the unadjusted series. The adjusted series turned 1.0 month earlier at the peak of Cycle I and 2.0 months earlier at the terminal trough of Cycle IV than did the unadjusted Southeast series. At each of these turning points the adjusted series showed greater United States-Southeast differences than was revealed for the unadjusted Southeast series, though all differences were quite small.

Duration of expansion in nonagricultural employment in the Southeast during Cycle I was shortened by 1.0 month and the duration of contraction lengthened by 1.0 month as the result of adjustment for industry-mix, but the full cycle duration of Cycle I was unaffected. The contraction and the full cycle of Cycle IV in Southeast nonagricultural employment were shortened by 2.0 months as the result of adjustment for industry composition. Again, the differences between the United States and the Southeast were slightly

TABLE 6-1
TURNING POINTS, DURATIONS, AND AMPLITUDES OF CYCLES IN NONAGRICULTURAL EMPLOYMENT,
UNITED STATES, SOUTHEAST UNADJUSTED, AND SOUTHEAST ADJUSTED

Cycle	Turning points Init. Trough	Peak	Term. Trough	S.E. lead (−) or lag (+) (months) Peak	Trough	Durations (months) Expan.	Contr.	Full Cycle	Amplitudes Expan.	Contr.	Full Cycle
Cycle I											
U.S.	9/45	8/48	10/49			35.0	14.0	49.0	14.0	−4.4	19.1
S.E., unadjusted	10/45	7/48	10/49	−1.0	0.0	33.0	15.0	48.0	15.8	−4.0	19.8
S.E., adjusted	10/45	6/48	10/49	−2.0	0.0	32.0	16.0	48.0	15.9	−4.1	20.0
Cycle II											
U.S.	10/49	7/53	8/54			45.0	13.0	58.0	15.0	−3.5	18.5
S.E., unadjusted	10/49	7/53	6/54	0.0	−2.0	45.0	11.0	56.0	17.9	−2.9	20.8
S.E., adjusted	10/49	7/53	6/54	0.0	−2.0	45.0	11.0	56.0	18.5	−2.5	21.0
Cycle III											
U.S.	8/54	4/57	5/58			32.0	13.0	45.0	8.2	−4.2	12.4
S.E., unadjusted	6/54	8/57	4/58	+4.0	−1.0	38.0	8.0	46.0	11.3	−2.2	13.5
S.E., adjusted	6/54	8/57	4/58	+4.0	−1.0	38.0	8.0	46.0	11.2	−2.1	13.3
Cycle IV											
U.S.	5/58	4/60	4/61			23.0	12.0	35.0	6.4	−1.6	8.0
S.E., unadjusted	4/58	4/60	4/61	0.0	0.0	24.0	12.0	36.0	6.9	−0.6	7.5
S.E., adjusted	4/58	4/60	2/61	0.0	−2.0	24.0	10.0	34.0	7.5	−0.7	8.2
Average[a]											
U.S.						33.8	13.0	46.8	11.1	−3.4	14.5
S.E., unadjusted				+0.8	−0.8	35.0	11.5	46.5	13.0	−2.4	15.4
S.E., adjusted				+0.5	−1.2	34.8	11.2	46.0	13.3	−2.3	15.6

[a] Each column averaged separately.
Sources: Data for U.S. and S.E., unadjusted, same as in Table 3-2. Figures for S.E., adjusted, derived by assigning appropriate weights to components of S.E. nonagricultural employment.

widened when industrial composition of the Southeast was
adjusted to conform to the country as a whole.

Amplitudes

Comparison of amplitudes of adjusted and unadjusted
Southeastern nonagricultural employment indicates that the
existing industrial make-up of this series in the Southeast
during the postwar period had a slight stabilizing effect
during periods of expansion and over the full cycle but
virtually no influence during contractions. The effect of
adjusting nonagricultural employment was generally an
accentuation of differences between the United States and
the Southeast in amplitudes of fluctuation—the contraction
and full-cycle amplitudes of Cycle IV were exceptions.

COMMODITY-PRODUCING EMPLOYMENT

Nonagricultural, commodity-producing employment in the
Southeast was adjusted for industry-mix by assigning appropriate weights to three component series: mining, contract
construction, and manufacturing employment. Quantitative
measures of the cyclical behavior of this hypothetical Southeastern series are presented in Table 6-2 and compared with
the unadjusted series for the Southeast and to the national
series. The unadjusted data for the Southeast and those for
the United States are identical to the information presented
in Table 4-1.

Timing and Durations

Comparison of the adjusted and unadjusted figures for
the Southeast shows only one divergence of turning points;
this occurred at the peak of Cycle III. At this point the
adjusted series turned 1.0 month later than the unadjusted
series. This difference in timing widened the differential
between the United States and the Southeast at this point,
though only by 1.0 month.

The single displaced turning point noted above had

TABLE 6-2

TURNING POINTS, DURATIONS, AND AMPLITUDES OF CYCLES IN COMMODITY-PRODUCING EMPLOYMENT, UNITED STATES, SOUTHEAST UNADJUSTED, AND SOUTHEAST ADJUSTED

Cycle	Turning points			S.E. lead (−) or lag (+) (months)		Durations (months)			Amplitudes	
	Init. Trough	Peak	Term. Trough	Peak	Trough	Expan.	Contr.	Full Cycle	Expan. Contr.	Full Cycle
Cycle I										
U.S.	10/45	7/48	10/49			33.0	15.0	48.0	19.0 — 9.5	28.5
S.E., unadjusted	11/45	6/48	10/49	−1.0	0.0	31.0	16.0	47.0	23.0 —11.4	31.7
S.E., adjusted	11/45	6/48	10/49	−1.0	0.0	31.0	16.0	47.0	19.0 —10.6	29.6
Cycle II										
U.S.	10/49	7/53	8/54			45.0	13.0	58.0	21.0 — 8.8	29.8
S.E., unadjusted	10/49	7/53	8/54	0.0	0.0	45.0	13.0	58.0	19.5 — 7.1	26.6
S.E., adjusted	10/49	7/53	8/54	0.0	0.0	45.0	13.0	58.0	19.7 — 6.5	26.2
Cycle III										
U.S.	8/54	2/57	6/58			30.0	16.0	46.0	8.2 —10.1	18.3
S.E., unadjusted	8/54	7/57	5/58	+5.0	−1.0	35.0	10.0	45.0	10.3 — 4.9	15.3
S.E., adjusted	8/54	8/57	5/58	+6.0	−1.0	36.0	9.0	45.0	9.5 — 4.5	14.0
Cycle IV										
U.S.	6/58	2/60	2/61			20.0	12.0	32.0	7.5 — 5.8	13.3
S.E., unadjusted	5/58	4/60	4/61	+2.0	+2.0	23.0	12.0	35.0	7.3 — 3.5	10.8
S.E., adjusted	5/58	4/60	4/61	+2.0	+2.0	23.0	12.0	35.0	8.0 — 3.3	11.3
Average[a]										
U.S.						32.0	14.0	46.0	13.9 — 8.6	22.5
S.E., unadjusted				+1.5	+0.2	33.5	12.8	46.3	14.4 — 6.7	21.1
S.E., adjusted				+1.8	+0.2	33.8	12.5	46.3	14.1 — 6.2	20.3

[a] Each column averaged separately.

Sources: Data for U.S. and S.E., unadjusted, same as in Table 4-1. Figures for S.E., adjusted, derived by assigning appropriate weights to components of S.E. commodity-producing employment.

little effect on the duration of the intracycle phases in the Southeast. Duration of expansion was 1.0 month longer and duration of contraction was 1.0 month shorter in the Southeast adjusted series than for the Southeast unadjusted series. The differences between the United States and the Southeast in duration during these two intracycle phases were widened by 1.0 month as a result of adjusting for industrial composition.

Amplitudes

Average amplitudes of fluctuations of Southeastern adjusted and unadjusted commodity-producing employment indicate that the industrial composition of this aggregate was responsible for the lack of stability in both the expansion and contraction phases. Examination of the individual cycles shows that—with the exception of the expansion amplitude of Cycle IV—amplitudes were larger for the unadjusted than for the adjusted series. This was true of the full-cycle amplitudes, also—with exception of Cycle IV.

SERVICES EMPLOYMENT

Employment in the services sector was adjusted for industrial composition by appropriately weighting five components according to their relative weight in the nation as a whole. These five components were transportation and public utilities, wholesale and retail trade, finance (including real estate and insurance), miscellaneous services, and state, local, and federal government. Examination of the resulting adjusted series of Southeastern services employment produced the cyclical information presented in Table 6-3. Also presented in this table are the same United States and Southeast data previously presented in Table 5-1.

Timing and Durations

The adjusted series for Southeast services employment revealed a terminal trough of Cycle III (or, initial trough of

TABLE 6-3

TURNING POINTS, DURATIONS, AND AMPLITUDES OF CYCLES IN SERVICES EMPLOYMENT, UNITED STATES, SOUTHEAST UNADJUSTED, AND SOUTHEAST ADJUSTED

	Turning points			S.E. lead (−) or lag (+) (months)		Durations (months)			Amplitudes		
	Init.	Peak	Term.					Full			Full
Cycle	Trough		Trough	Peak	Trough	Expan.	Contr.	Cycle	Expan.	Contr.	Cycle
Cycle I											
U.S.	9/45	12/48	11/49			39.0	11.0	50.0	13.7	−0.8	14.5
S.E., unadjusted	10/45	11/48	11/49	−1.0	0.0	37.0	12.0	49.0	14.0	−0.6	14.6
S.E., adjusted	10/45	11/48	11/49	−1.0	0.0	37.0	12.0	49.0	15.3	−0.6	15.9
Cycle II											
U.S.	11/49	10/53	3/54			47.0	5.0	52.0	11.1	−0.3	11.4
S.E., unadjusted	11/49	10/53	3/54	0.0	0.0	47.0	5.0	52.0	17.2	−0.1	17.3
S.E., adjusted	11/49	10/53	3/54	0.0	0.0	47.0	5.0	52.0	18.0	−0.1	18.1
Cycle III											
U.S.	3/54	8/57	4/58			41.0	8.0	49.0	9.4	−1.2	10.6
S.E., unadjusted	3/54	9/57	6/58	+1.0	+2.0	42.0	9.0	51.0	12.1	−0.2	12.3
S.E., adjusted	3/54	9/57	4/58	+1.0	0.0	42.0	7.0	49.0	12.4	−0.5	12.9
Cycle IV											
U.S.	4/58	11/60	4/61			31.0	5.0	36.0	6.6	−0.1	6.7
S.E., unadjusted	6/58	11/60	2/61	0.0	−2.0	29.0	3.0	32.0	7.5	−0.1	7.6
S.E., adjusted	4/58	11/60	2/61	0.0	−2.0	31.0	3.0	34.0	7.9	−0.1	8.0
Average[a]											
U.S.						39.5	7.3	46.8	10.2	−0.6	10.8
S.E., unadjusted				0.0	0.0	38.8	7.3	46.0	12.7	−0.3	13.0
S.E., adjusted				0.0	−0.5	39.2	6.8	46.0	13.4	−0.3	13.7

[a] Each column averaged separately.

Sources: Data for U.S. and S.E., unadjusted, same as in Table 5-1. Figures for S.E., adjusted, derived by assigning appropriate weights to components of S.E. services employment.

Cycle IV) 2.0 months earlier than did the unadjusted series. This was the only difference in timing between the two Southeast's series. Unlike the differences in timing as a result of standardizing the Southeast region noted for the two previous series examined, this difference in timing brought the United States and Southeast closer together with respect to this particular trough.

Since the difference in timing between the adjusted and unadjusted series for the Southeast occurred at a mutual trough, its influence on duration was reflected in two cycles. The duration of contraction and the full-cycle duration of Cycle III were both 2.0 months shorter and the expansion duration and full-cycle duration of Cycle I were 2.0 months longer for adjusted Southeastern services employment than for the corresponding unadjusted Southeast series.

Amplitudes

Amplitudes of fluctuation for the adjusted and unadjusted Southeast series of services employment indicate that the particular industry-mix of this aggregate series had a stabilizing effect during expansions, but the differences between amplitudes during contractions were hardly noticeable —in fact, the average amplitudes were identical. Again, the differences between the United States and the Southeast were accentuated during expansion and the full cycle after the series was adjusted for industry-mix.

MANUFACTURING EMPLOYMENT

Southeast manufacturing employment was adjusted by weighting durable- and nondurable-gods manufacturing according to their weight in the country as a whole. Examination of this aggregate series for the Southeast was limited to only two complete cycles and only ten of the twelve Southeastern states because data were unavailable for a more complete analysis. Quantitative measures concerning the cyclical behavior of this hypothetical series are shown in Table 6-4.

TABLE 6-4

TURNING POINTS, DURATIONS, AND AMPLITUDES OF CYCLES IN MANUFACTURING EMPLOYMENT, UNITED STATES, SOUTHEAST UNADJUSTED, AND SOUTHEAST ADJUSTED[a]

Cycle	Turning points			S.E. lead (−) or lag (+) (months)		Durations (months)			Amplitudes		
	Init. Trough	Peak	Term. Trough	Peak	Trough	Expan.	Contr.	Full Cycle	Expan.	Contr.	Full Cycle
Cycle III											
U.S.	8/54	3/57	5/58			31.0	14.0	45.0	+ 7.4	−10.1	17.5
S.E., unadjusted	7/54	4/57	4/58	+1.0	−1.0	33.0	12.0	45.0	+ 9.5	− 4.1	13.6
S.E., adjusted	6/54	7/57	5/58	+4.0	0.0	37.0	10.0	47.0	+11.1	− 5.2	16.3
Cycle IV											
U.S.	5/58	2/60	2/61			21.0	12.0	33.0	+ 8.3	− 6.2	14.5
S.E., unadjusted	4/58	4/60	2/61	+2.0	0.0	24.0	10.0	34.0	+10.9	− 3.4	14.3
S.E., adjusted	5/58	4/60	2/61	+2.0	0.0	23.0	10.0	33.0	+13.7	− 5.1	18.8
Average[b]											
U.S.						30.8	15.3	46.0	+13.3	− 9.2	22.5
S.E., unadjusted				+1.5	−0.5	28.5	11.0	39.5	+10.2	− 3.8	14.0
S.E., adjusted				+3.0	0.0	30.0	10.0	40.0	+12.4	− 5.2	17.6

[a] S.E., both adjusted and unadjusted, includes only ten states.
[b] Each column averaged separately.

Sources: Data for U.S. same as in Table 4-4. Figures for S.E., adjusted, derived by assigning appropriate weights to S.E. durable-goods and nondurable-goods manufacturing employment.

The figures for the United States presented in this table are identical to those presented in Table 4-4. However, the figures for the Southeast, unadjusted, represent the unadjusted figures for the same ten states included in the adjusted series. This was necessary in order to maintain comparability between the two Southeast series.

Timing and Durations

The Southeast adjusted and unadjusted manufacturing employment series differed in timing at each of the three turning points of Cycle III. Southeast manufacturing employment adjusted for composition turned 1.0 month earlier at the initial trough, 3.0 months later at the peak and 1.0 month later at the terminal trough than did the Southeast unadjusted series. Table 6-4 also shows a difference in timing between the two Southeast series at the initial trough of Cycle IV but it does not constitute a separate case inasmuch as this and the terminal trough of Cycle III are the same.

During Cycle III, duration of expansion was 4.0 months longer for adjusted Southeast manufacturing employment than for the unadjusted Southeast series; duration of contraction was 2.0 months shorter and the full-cycle duration was 2.0 months longer for the adjusted manufacturing employment series. In Cycle IV the expansion and full-cycle durations were 1.0 month shorter in the Southeast as a result of adjustment for industry-mix. During Cycle III adjustment for industrial composition widened the differences between the United States and the Southeast in durations but had the opposite effect during Cycle IV.

Amplitudes

Comparison of amplitudes of adjusted and unadjusted Southeastern manufacturing employment indicates that the particular industry-mix in the Southeast had a definite stabilizing effect during the last two postwar cycles. Amplitudes of the adjusted series were larger than those of the unadjusted series for all of the intracycle phases and the full cycles. Such a result, of course, could be expected since Southeastern manufacturing has a smaller proportion of the more volatile durable-goods industries than does national manufacturing.

CONCLUSIONS

Availability of detailed industry data permitted "standardization" of only four Southeastern employment series. These were employment in nonagricultural, commodity-producing, services, and manufacturing industries. Timing, duration, and amplitudes of these four hypothetical series were compared with the corresponding series for the United States as a whole and with the unadjusted Southeastern series in an effort to determine the cyclical influence of industry-mix in the Southeast.

Differences in timing and duration between the Southeastern adjusted and unadjusted series were usually quite small, particularly when averages were compared. The largest differences between the two Southeastern series occurred in manufacturing employment. Southeastern adjusted series generally revealed slightly larger differentials between the United States and the Southeast with respect to timing and duration than previously noted between the United States and the unadjusted Southeastern series.

Comparison of amplitudes of fluctuations in the Southeastern adjusted and unadjusted series revealed divergencies which were relatively quite small, with the exception of manufacturing employment. The evidence indicates that the industry-mix of Southeastern nonagricultural industries had a slightly stabilizing effect on the cyclical fluctuations of employment in this region. Nonagricultural employment was the most highly aggregated series adjusted for industrial composition; the other three series were, in fact, components of total nonagricultural employment. Consequently, the evidence revealed through examination of total nonagricultural employment is the key to any broad generalizations concerning the effect of the Southeast's industry-mix on the cyclical behavior of employment.

Commodity-producing and services industries are the two major components of nonagricultural industries. Comparison of amplitudes of fluctuation for these two adjusted and unadjusted employment series indicated that the industrial composition of Southeastern services was slightly stabilizing while the converse appeared to be true of commodity-producing industries.

The commodity-producing sector was disaggregated into three components: contract construction, mining, and manufacturing employment. The stabilizing effect of the industry-mix of commodity-producing industries, with respect to Southeastern employment, can be attributed to Southeastern contract construction industries and, perhaps to a lesser degree, to Southeastern mining industries. It was noted previously (Chapter IV) that employment in these two industries was more volatile in the Southeast than in the nation as a whole. This was particularly true of contract construction. And it has been observed in this chapter that the industry-mix of Southeastern manufacturing (the third component of the commodity-producing sector) was clearly stabilizing with respect to fluctuations in employment.

The stability of Southeastern manufacturing industries was, no doubt, due to the greater relative weight of the less volatile nondurable-goods industries in this region.

7

CONCLUSION

*T*HE PRIMARY objective of this study has been to analyze and compare selected corresponding income and employment series in the Southeast and in the United States as a whole in an effort to isolate the relative cyclical behavior of the Southeastern region of the United States. Comparisons were made of turning points, durations, and cycle amplitudes. In addition to comparing the cyclical behavior of a particular series in the Southeast with the corresponding series in the United States as a whole, disaggregated series for the Southeast were compared with their parent series and with other appropriate component series

(Southeastern and national) in a further effort to isolate any peculiar behavior of income and employment in the Southeast.

Nineteen income and employment series for the Southeast and the United States were analyzed and compared over the postwar period. Because of deficiencies in data, the aggregate nonagricultural employment series was the only one of these series which could be disaggregated into its various components. This series was first divided into two major sectors: commodity-producing industries and services industries. The commodity-producing sector was then disaggregated into mining, contract construction, and manufacturing industries. And, since manufacturing employment included such a large part of the total commodity-producing sector, this series was further divided into durable-goods and nondurable-goods manufacturing industries. Average weekly hours of production workers in manufacturing were also analyzed in connection with manufacturing employment. The services sector was disaggregated into five components: employment in transportation and public utilities, wholesale and retail trade, finance, services and miscellaneous, and government industries.

SUMMARY OF FINDINGS

Income

The only noticeable difference between the cyclical behavior of personal income in the Southeast and the United States was in the size of amplitudes. Personal income in the Southeast revealed larger average amplitudes than its national counterpart during the full cycle and both intracycle phases.

Per capita personal income also revealed greater amplitudes of fluctuations in the Southeast than in the United States over the complete cycle and both intracycle phases. There was some indication that the percentage of national population residing in the Southeast declined more rapidly during recessions than during expansions but this did not appreciably influence the relative cyclical behavior of Southeastern per capita personal income.[1]

Cash receipts from farm marketings in the Southeast revealed amplitudes of expansion, contraction, and the full cycle which were considerably larger than amplitudes of the corresponding national series. This series was also more volatile than either of the other income series examined.

Average weekly earnings of production workers in manufacturing revealed turning points at about the same time in the Southeast as in the United States. Furthermore, cyclical durations and amplitudes were roughly the same for this series in both areas.

The greater volatility and greater weight of farm income in the Southeast appears to be the primary cause of the relative instability of Southeastern personal income and per capita personal income. This is further substantiated by the greater instability of Southeastern agricultural employment.

Aggregate Employment

Southeastern agricultural employment showed turning points identical with those in United States agricultural employment. Amplitudes, however, were larger for agricultural employment in the Southeast during expansions, contractions, and the full cycle.

Differences in timing of turning points and durations of cycles and intracycle phases of total *non*agricultural employment in the Southeast and the United States were confined to only one cycle. This difference in timing and duration was apparently created by employment in the commodity-producing sector. Although differences between cyclical durations of Southeastern and United States nonagricultural employment were generally insignificant, the average expan-

[1] The percentage of national population residing in the Southeast has declined slightly over the postwar years. The ratio decreased most markedly during postwar recessions, with the exception of the 1957-1958 recession.

sion duration was longer and the average contraction duration was shorter for this type employment in the Southeast.

Total nonagricultural employment revealed stronger expansions in the Southeast than in the United States, and these stronger expansions more than offset the weaker contractions in the Southeast, causing the full-cycle amplitudes to be larger in the Southeast. The stronger expansions in Southeastern total nonagricultural employment are primarily due to stronger expansions in employment in the Southeastern services sector; the weaker contractions in Southeastern total nonagricultural employment resulted from the weaker contractions in employment in the services sector and manufacturing employment of the commodity-producing sector.

Commodity-Producing Employment

There was only one significant difference in the timing of turning points of employment in Southeastern commodity-producing industries and its national counterpart. This difference and the resulting difference in duration was created by a difference in the timing of Southeastern contract construction employment compared with its national counterpart. While Southeastern contract construction employment created the differences observed for the parent sectors, in one instance it *prevented* a difference in timing from appearing in the parent sectors—by offsetting a difference in timing between manufacturing employment in the Southeast and manufacturing employment in the United States.

Overall, employment in Southeastern commodity-producing industries was *more* stable than the corresponding series in the United States. The average full-cycle amplitude of employment in commodity-producing industries was smaller for the Southeast than for the United States. The average contraction amplitude was also smaller for the Southeast and the average expansion amplitude was only slightly larger for the Southeast than for the United States.

The greater stability of employment in Southeastern

commodity-producing industries was clearly created by Southeastern manufacturing employment, which can be attributed to the greater weight of nondurable-goods manufacturing in the Southeast.

Services Employment

Turning points of employment in services industries were virtually the same for the Southeast and the United States. The average amplitudes of Southeastern services employment were larger during expansion and the full cycle and smaller during contraction than their respective national counterparts. The larger expansion and full-cycle amplitudes for the Southeast reflect the joint behavior of all five of the component series. All five components contributed to the instability of the services sector in the Southeast during expansions and over the full cycles, but the *stability* of services employment in the Southeast during recessions was created by the greater stability of Southeastern employment in transportation, trade, and government industries.

Effect of Industry-Mix

Four nonagricultural employment series for the Southeast were adjusted so that the region's industrial composition would conform to that of the country as a whole. These hypothetical series were then examined for cyclical movement and compared with the corresponding unadjusted Southeastern series and with the corresponding national series. The four employment series adjusted for composition were nonagricultural employment, commodity-producing employment, services employment, and manufacturing employment. The latter is a component of commodity-producing employment.

The adjustment for industry-mix altered only very slightly the relative cyclical behavior of Southeastern nonagricultural employment. Total nonagricultural employment was more stable before the adjustment was made. Of the two major components of nonagricultural employment, total services employment was more stable before adjustment and total commodity-producing employment was more stable after adjustment. Manufacturing employment, a component of commodity-producing employment, was more stable before adjustment for industry-mix, which can be explained by the greater weight of nondurables in the Southeast.

CONCLUSIONS

Cyclical Performance

This investigation indicates that forces which precipitated cyclical perturbations in a given type of income or employment during the postwar period were felt at approximately the same time in the Southeast as in the nation as a whole. Consequently, the durations of full cycles and intra-cycle phases for particular Southeastern income or employment series were not appreciably different from the corresponding series in the United States. Although overall interareal differences in timing were not substantial, there was a tendency for aggregate nonagricultural employment and the disaggregated nonagricultural employment series to reveal slightly longer periods of expansion and slightly shorter periods of contraction in the Southeast than in the United States. It was the persistency, not the magnitude, of this behavior that warrants its attention.

Income and employment do not encompass the complete economic activity of the Southeastern region. Therefore, it is impossible to determine whether the entire Southeastern economy was more or less sensitive to cyclical swings than the national economy. Perhaps the best basis for approximating the overall stability of the Southeast is the relative size of expansion, contraction, and full-cycle amplitudes in the broadest aggregates examined. These aggregates were personal income, agricultural employment, and nonagricultural employment. Each of these series reveals larger average full-cycle amplitudes for the Southeast than for the nation, though the difference was quite small for nonagricultural employment. This suggests greater instability in the Southeast during the postwar period.

A comparison of intracycle amplitudes of fluctuations in the aggregate income and employment series indicates that the Southeast was also relatively less stable during the postwar cyclical expansions. During postwar cyclical contractions, personal income and agricultural employment in the Southeast revealed greater declines than did these aggregates in the United States; however, Southeastern nonagricultural employment showed the opposite relative behavior.

Relative to their respective national counterparts, Southeastern income was less stable than Southeastern employment; and Southeastern agricultural employment was less stable than Southeastern nonagricultural employment. In general this was true whether viewed from full-cycle amplitudes or from intracycle amplitudes.

The greater instability of Southeastern personal income (and per capita personal income) was attributed primarily to the greater weight and greater volatility of Southeastern farm income. Factors other than those examined in this study, however, may have contributed to the relative instability of personal income in the Southeast. Results of a previous study indicate that proprietors income, both farm and nonfarm, is one of the most volatile of the major sources of personal income.[2] As a percentage of total personal income, proprietors income is larger in the Southeast than in the nation as a whole. Although the interareal differences in the cyclical behavior of this type of income are not known, the greater relative weight in the Southeast prompts me to speculate that proprietors income contributed to the relative instability of Southeastern personal income.

Employment in small firms is more variable than in large firms,[3] and the greater relative importance of small

[2] Daniel Creamer, *Personal Income during Business Cycles* (Princeton: Princeton University Press, 1956), 111-12.

[3] Charles E. Ferguson, "The Relationship of Business Size to Stability: An Empirical Approach," *Journal of Industrial Economics*, IX (November 1960), 43-62.

firms in the Southeast may be another factor contributing to this region's instability. This factor should affect both income and employment. But nonagricultural employment was more stable in the Southeast than in the United States during contractions, which is contrary to what one would expect if firm size played a significant role in determining cyclical differences between the two regions. The greater number of small farms, however, is probably the most important factor determining the greater instability of Southeastern agricultural employment. Less diversification in Southeastern agriculture must also be considered, and this can never be overcome completely because the United States as a whole will always be more diversified than any single region.

There are many other factors which underlie the cyclical movements of a region and the disproportional weights of these factors contribute to interregional differences in cycles. The proportion of skilled workers in the labor force, the strength of unions, and state and local fiscal policies are but a few. However, the cyclical importance of these factors in the Southeast is difficult to assay.

Growth Implications

The nature of this study prevents any testing of the "growth-stability" hypothesis discussed in Chapter I.[4] It was noted, however, that the general behavior of amplitudes in the Southeast relative to their counterparts in the United States was contrary to what would be expected. The expected behavior was based on the assumption that the Southeast was indeed a slow-growth region during the postwar period and that, consequently, expansion amplitudes

[4] In order to test the "growth-stability" hypothesis, it would be necessary to make a "reasonably" accurate measure of the trend or growth rate of the Southeast and the United States. As mentioned previously, the postwar period is probably too short to make such a measure. Furthermore, the procedure used for computing cycle amplitudes in this study eliminates only the intercycle trend from a particular series. Thus, the amplitudes may be affected to some extent by the intracycle trend of a particular series.

would be smaller, contraction amplitudes larger, and full-cycle amplitudes larger for the Southeast.

There are two possible explanations for the apparent contradiction. First, the hypothesis that more slowly growing regions will display the type of cyclical behavior noted has not, itself, been sufficiently tested. Secondly, although the period covered was too short really to measure relative growth, many of the series analyzed increased faster in the Southeast than in the nation as a whole, and most increased at least as fast. This cyclical analysis indicates that Southeastern nonagricultural employment (and most of its components) sprinted along at a faster rate than its national counterpart during expansions and declined less during contractions. The faster rate, plus the fact that average durations of expansion were generally slightly longer and average durations of contractions were generally slightly shorter for Southeastern nonagricultural employment, raises some questions about the applicability of the slow-growth label to the Southeastern nonagricultural sector during the more recent postwar years.[5]

These conclusions with respect to the relative cyclical and growth performance of the Southeast during the postwar period are not altered when amplitudes are expressed on a per month basis;[6] nor does comparison of the Southeastern income and employment series with their non-Southeastern counterparts change the general conclusions.[7]

Cyclical Outlook

The declining importance of agriculture as a source of income and employment in the Southeast and the increasing diversification of Southeastern agriculture are favorable movements. Mining in the Southeast is also declining more

---

[5] This reasoning is valid only when trend is not eliminated from the series, as was the case in this analysis.

[6] See L. R. McGee and S. S. Goodman, "Postwar Cyclical Fluctuations in Income and Employment: Southeast and United States," *Southern Economic Journal*, XXXI (April 1965), 298-313.

[7] See Appendix B.

rapidly than in the United States, but the importance of mining as a source of income and employment is quite small and will have very little effect on the relative cyclical behavior of the Southeast in the future. The Southeast is making relative gains in the more stable services industries and the gains in commodity-producing industries are usually in the form of highly efficient plants. The Southeast is also improving its relative position with respect to professional and technical workers, and is not so dependent on proprietors income as it was during the early postwar years.

These are some of the cyclically favorable trends in the Southeast and they are also favorable for future growth. Whether or not they will be outweighed by unfavorable factors remains to be seen. One thing is sure: it is not likely that the Southeast will ever have the same cyclical response as the nation as a whole (or other regions), for national cycles represent the joint cyclical movements of all regions. And the composite of forces which underlie regional cycles will differ among regions.

APPENDIX A

SOURCES OF DATA

Only those income and employment series which were available on a monthly basis for the Southeast and the United States were used in this analysis. It was necessary that monthly data be used to compare timing and duration of cycles. The paucity of monthly figures for the individual states, or the Southeast region, placed some limitations on the number of series which could be used. This was particularly true of the income series, for there were no reliable state income figures available by industry, with the exception of average weekly earnings of production workers in manufacturing. The following series were used for the investigation because they were available monthly and were reasonably comparable for the Southeast and the nation as a whole:

(1) personal income
(2) per capita personal income
(3) cash receipts from farm marketings
(4) total agricultural employment
(5) total nonagricultural employment
(6) employment in commodity-producing industries

(7) employment in services industries
(8) mining employment
(9) contract-construction employment
(10) manufacturing employment
(11) durable-goods manufacturing employment
(12) nondurable-goods manufacturing employment
(13) average weekly *earnings* of production workers in manufacturing
(14) average weekly *hours* of production workers in manufacturing
(15) employment in transportation and public utilities
(16) employment in wholesale and retail trade
(17) employment in finance
(18) employment in services and miscellaneous industries
(19) employment in state, local, and federal government

Income

The personal income figures used in the present study were those published by *Business Week*.[1] These figures only go back to 1947. But this is the only source which reports personal income by month for the individual states. The *Business Week* figures were compared to the annual figures reported by the U. S. Department of Commerce and the largest error noted was 2.7 percent.[2] This is not surprising

[1] Personal income figures for the period 1947-1958 were published in a supplement to *Business Week*, March 28, 1959. Monthly personal income figures since 1958 are published each month in one of the regular issues of *Business Week*.

[2] Comparisons were made for the United States, the Southeastern region, and the individual Southeastern states. The figures published by the U. S. Department of Commerce were used as a base. These figures were divided into the difference between the annual personal income figures published by *Business Week* and those published by the U. S. Department of Commerce. The "error" was computed for each year for the period 1947-1961. For the U. S. Department of Commerce personal income figures, see U.S. Bureau of the Census, *Personal*

since the data reported by *Business Week* are periodically adjusted to U. S. Department of Commerce benchmarks.

Per capita personal income was computed by using the personal income data from *Business Week* and population estimates from the Bureau of the Census.[3] Since monthly population estimates are not published for individual states, it was necessary to prorate the annual change over the twelve months. To make the per capita personal income data more comparable, the United States figures were adjusted using the same method.[4]

Average weekly earnings of production workers in manufacturing were taken from *Employment and Earnings*, and from the reports prepared by the cooperating state agencies.[5] These average weekly earnings figures are "gross."[6]

Cash receipts from farm marketings were obtained from various issues of *Farm Income Situation*.[7] This series includes gross receipts from the sale of all farm products, net loans

---

Income by State Since 1929 (Washington, D.C.: U. S. Government Printing Office, 1956). Since 1956 annual personal income figures by state and for the United States are published in the August issues of U. S. Bureau of the Census, *Survey of Current Business*.

[3] U. S. Bureau of the Census, *Current Population Reports, P-25 Series*.

[4] Monthly population figures for the United States are reported in the above source. However, to maintain comparability between the per capita personal income series for the United States and the Southeast, annual population estimates were prorated over the twelve months for both areas.

[5] Most of the states have an agency which prepares monthly employment and earnings reports for their particular state in cooperation with the Bureau of Labor Statistics. Most of the employment and earnings data for the Southeastern region were obtained from the reports prepared by the twelve Southeastern state agencies. For names and addresses of these agencies, see the inside back cover of any recent monthly issue of U. S. Department of Labor, *Employment and Earnings*.

[6] "Gross" average weekly earnings of production workers in manufacturing include earnings of part-time workers as well as earnings of full-time workers. Gross average weekly earnings are influenced by changes in gross average *hourly* earnings, length of the workweek, part-time work, labor turnover, absenteeism, and work stoppage of any kind. See *ibid*.

[7] U. S. Department of Agriculture, *Farm Income Situation*.

made or guaranteed by the Commodity Credit Corporation, and purchases under price support programs.[8]

Employment

All nonagricultural employment and hour data for the United States as a whole were taken from *Employment and Earnings*.[9] All nonagricultural data for the Southeastern states for the period 1951-1961 came from reports prepared for the Bureau of Labor Statistics by cooperating state agencies.[10] For the period 1945-1950, nonagricultural data for the Southeastern states were taken from *State Employment, 1939-56*.[11] The nonagricultural employment data did not include military personnel, proprietors, self-employed, unpaid family workers, or domestic workers.

Agricultural employment figures for the nation and the Southeast were estimates published by the U. S. Department of Agriculture in *Farm Labor* and *Farm Employment*.[12] Agricultural employment included family workers and hired workers. Workers under fourteen years of age were included and there is some unavoidable double counting of persons working on more than one farm.

The agricultural employment figures were not strictly comparable to the total employment and nonagricultural employment estimates of the Bureau of Labor Statistics. They differed in that the estimates of the Bureau of Labor Statistics did not include workers under fourteen years of age and contained no double counting of dual jobholders or unpaid family workers. They also differed in that different techniques of sampling were used. The estimates of agricul-

[8] *Ibid.*

[9] U. S. Department of Labor, *Employment and Earnings*, Bulletin 1312 (Washington, D.C.: U. S. Government Printing Office, 1961).

[10] See note 5 above.

[11] U. S. Department of Labor, *State Employment, 1939-56* (Washington, D.C.: U. S. Government Printing Office, 1957).

[12] U. S. Department of Agriculture, *Farm Labor*, January 1960 and January 1961; U. S. Department of Agriculture, *Farm Employment*, Statistical Bulletin 236 (Washington, D.C.: U. S. Department of Agriculture, 1958).

tural employment by the U. S. Department of Agriculture were probably higher than those of the Bureau of Labor Statistics which were included in the estimates of *total* employment. Monthly agricultural employment figures were not published by the Bureau of Labor Statistics for the individual states; consequently, there was no way to check the actual differences. The lack of comparability did not create any serious problem since, primarily, comparison was made between Southeastern agricultural employment and United States agricultural employment. And agricultural employment data used for the Southeast and the United States were estimates of the U. S. Department of Agriculture.

All of the series, with exception of personal income, were seasonally adjusted by the author.[13] Personal income figures (also used in computing per capita personal income) were seasonally adjusted by *Business Week*.

[13] The seasonal adjustment method used was the X-8 electronic generator computer method developed by the Bureau of the Census. This method is explained in Julius Shiskin, "Electronic Computer Seasonal Adjustments, Test and Revision of U. S. Census Methods," in *Seasonal Adjustment on Electronic Computers*, Proceedings of an International Conference held in Paris, November 1961 (Paris: Organization for Economic Co-operation and Development, 1961), pp. 79-150.

APPENDIX B

SOUTHEAST AND NON-SOUTHEAST

Comparing a specific regional series with its national counterpart, such as the previous comparisons made in this study, is somewhat analogous to comparing a specific national series to the reference cycle. This appendix carries the analysis one step further by comparing the cyclical behavior of Southeastern income and employment with their respective counterparts in the non-Southeast (see Tables B1-14). The non-Southeast region does not directly reflect the influence of the Southeast region whereas this was not true of the nation as a whole. Consequently, comparison of the Southeast with the non-Southeast may isolate additional cyclical characteristics peculiar to the Southeast; at least, it should further substantiate the relative cyclical characteristics previously observed for the Southeast.

Not all of the series examined previously are analyzed and compared in this chapter. Not included here are per capita personal income, employment in durable-goods industries, employment in nondurable-goods industries, average weekly hours of production workers in manufacturing, and average weekly earnings of production workers in manufacturing. Suitable data pertaining to the above series were not available for the non-Southeast region. All the series re-examined revealed a greater percentage increase over the postwar period for the Southeast than for the non-Southeast except agricultural employment and mining employment; the latter two series decreased at a greater rate in the Southeast.

Comparison of income and employment series for the Southeast with their counterparts for the non-Southeast revealed essentially the same *relative* cyclical behavior for the Southeast as previously observed in Southeast-United States comparisons. The margin of difference was generally wider between the Southeast and the non-Southeast than between the Southeast and the United States as a whole; however, these differences were generally in the same direction and the causes of these divergencies appeared to be the same in both comparisons.

TABLE B-1
TURNING POINTS, DURATIONS, AND AMPLITUDES OF CYCLES IN TOTAL PERSONAL INCOME, SOUTHEAST AND NON-SOUTHEAST

Cycle	Turning points			S.E. lead (−) or lag (+) (months)		Durations (months)			Amplitudes		
	Init. Trough	Peak	Term. Trough	Peak	Trough	Expan.	Contr.	Full Cycle	Expan.	Contr.	Full Cycle
Cycle I											
Non-S.E.	(a)	9/48	8/49			(a)	11.0	(a)	(a)	−3.3	(a)
S.E.	(a)	10/48	8/49	+1.0	0.0	(a)	10.0	(a)	(a)	−5.9	(a)
Cycle II											
Non-S.E.	8/49	7/53	12/53			47.0	5.0	52.0	+32.6	−1.1	33.7
S.E.	8/49	7/53	12/53	0.0	0.0	47.0	5.0	52.0	+35.1	−1.1	36.2
Cycle III											
Non-S.E.	12/53	8/57	12/57			44.0	4.0	48.0	+20.7	−0.9	21.6
S.E.	12/53	8/57	12/57	0.0	0.0	44.0	4.0	48.0	+23.7	−4.0	27.7
Cycle IV											
Non-S.E.	12/57	7/60	1/61			31.0	6.0	37.0	+16.1	−1.5	17.6
S.E.	12/57	7/60	1/61	0.0	0.0	31.0	6.0	37.0	+19.9	−2.1	22.0
Average[b]											
Non-S.E.						40.7	5.0	45.7	+23.1	−1.2	24.3
S.E.				+0.3	0.0	40.7	5.0	45.7	+26.2	−2.4	28.6

[a] Data not available. [b] Each column averaged separately.
Source: See Appendix A.

TABLE B-2
TURNING POINTS, DURATIONS, AND AMPLITUDES OF CYCLES IN CASH RECEIPTS FROM FARM MARKETINGS, SOUTHEAST AND NON-SOUTHEAST

Cycle	Turning points			S.E. lead (−) or lag (+) (months)		Durations (months)			Amplitudes		
	Init. Trough	Peak	Term. Trough	Peak	Trough	Expan.	Contr.	Full Cycle	Expan.	Contr.	Full Cycle
Cycle II											
Non-S.E.	(a)	5/53	7/55			(a)	26.0	(a)	(a)	− 9.4	(a)
S.E.		3/53	11/54	−2.0	−8.0	(a)	20.0	(a)	(a)	−13.6	(a)
Cycle III											
Non-S.E.	7/55	10/56	6/57			15.0	8.0	23.0	+ 6.0	− 1.2	7.2
S.E.	11/54	10/56	9/57	0.0	+3.0	23.0	11.0	34.0	+16.2	−19.1	35.3
Cycle IV											
Non-S.E.	6/57	1/59	1/60			19.0	12.0	31.0	+13.4	− 6.7	20.1
S.E.	9/57	7/59	1/60	+6.0	0.0	22.0	6.0	28.0	+22.5	−12.3	34.8
Average[b]											
Non-S.E.						17.0	10.0	27.0	9.7	4.0	13.7
S.E.				+1.3	−1.7	22.5	8.5	31.0	19.4	15.7	35.1

[a] Data not available. [b] Each column averaged separately.
Source: See Appendix A.

TABLE B-3
TURNING POINTS, DURATIONS, AND AMPLITUDES OF CYCLES IN AGRICULTURAL EMPLOYMENT,
SOUTHEAST AND NON-SOUTHEAST

Cycle	Turning points			S.E. lead (−) or lag (+) (months)		Durations (months)			Amplitudes	
	Init. Trough	Peak	Term. Trough	Peak	Trough	Expan.	Contr.	Full Cycle	Expan. Contr.	Full Cycle
Cycle III										
Non-S.E.	12/53	10/55	12/56			22.0	14.0	36.0	−6.0 — 5.8	0.2
S.E.	12/53	10/55	12/56	0.0	0.0	22.0	14.0	36.0	−3.3 —11.3	8.3
Cycle IV										
Non-S.E.	12/56	3/59	8/60			27.0	17.0	44.0	−2.0 — 4.9	2.9
S.E.	12/56	3/59	8/60	0.0	0.0	27.0	17.0	44.0	−1.1 —10.6	9.5
Average[a]										
Non-S.E.						24.5	15.5	40.0	−4.1 — 5.4	1.6
S.E.				0.0	0.0	24.5	15.5	40.0	−2.2 —11.0	8.9

[a] Each column averaged separately.
Source: See Appendix A.

TABLE B-4
TURNING POINTS, DURATIONS, AND AMPLITUDES OF CYCLES IN NONAGRICULTURAL
EMPLOYMENT, SOUTHEAST AND NON-SOUTHEAST

Cycle	Turning points			S.E. lead (—) or lag (+) (months)		Durations (months)			Amplitudes		
	Init. Trough	Peak	Term. Trough	Peak	Trough	Expan.	Contr.	Full Cycle	Expan.	Contr.	Full Cycle
Cycle I											
Non-S.E.	9/45	8/48	10/49			33.0	14.0	47.0	+14.8	—4.5	19.3
S.E.	10/45	7/48	10/49	—1.0	0.0	33.0	15.0	48.0	+15.8	—4.0	19.8
Cycle II											
Non-S.E.	10/49	7/53	8/54			45.0	9.0	54.0	+14.5	—3.6	18.1
S.E.	10/49	7/53	6/54	0.0	—2.0	45.0	11.0	56.0	+17.9	—2.9	20.8
Cycle III											
Non-S.E.	8/54	3/57	5/58			31.0	14.0	45.0	+ 7.7	—4.8	12.5
S.E.	6/54	8/57	4/58	+5.0	—1.0	38.0	8.0	46.0	+11.3	—2.2	13.5
Cycle IV											
Non-S.E.	5/58	4/60	4/61			25.0	12.0	37.0	+ 6.3	—1.9	8.2
S.E.	4/58	4/60	4/61	0.0	0.0	24.0	12.0	36.0	+ 6.9	—0.6	7.5
Average[a]											
Non-S.E.						33.5	12.3	45.8	+10.8	—3.7	14.5
S.E.				+1.0	—0.8	35.0	11.5	46.5	+13.0	—2.4	15.4

[a] Each column averaged separately.
Source: See Appendix A.

TABLE B-5

Turning Points, Durations, and Amplitudes of Cycles in Employment in the Commodity-Producing Sector, Southeast and Non-Southeast

Cycle	Turning points			S.E. lead (—) or lag (+) (months)		Durations (months)			Amplitudes		
	Init. Trough	Peak	Term. Trough	Peak	Trough	Expan.	Contr.	Full Cycle	Expan.	Contr.	Full Cycle
Cycle I											
Non-S.E.	9/45	10/48	10/49			37.0	12.0	49.0	+15.9 — 9.6	25.5
S.E.	11/45	6/48	10/49	—4.0	0.0	31.0	16.0	47.0	+20.3 —11.4	31.7
Cycle II											
Non-S.E.	10/49	7/53	8/54			45.0	13.0	58.0	+21.1 — 9.1	30.2
S.E.	10/49	7/53	8/54	0.0	0.0	45.0	13.0	58.0	+19.5 — 7.1	26.6
Cycle III											
Non-S.E.	8/54	2/57	6/58			30.0	16.0	46.0	+ 8.0 —11.2	19.2
S.E.	8/54	7/57	5/58	+5.0	—1.0	35.0	10.0	45.0	+10.3 — 4.9	15.2
Cycle IV											
Non-S.E.	6/58	2/60	2/61			20.0	12.0	32.0	+ 7.7 — 6.5	14.2
S.E.	5/58	4/60	4/61	+2.0	+2.0	23.0	12.0	35.0	+ 7.3 — 3.5	10.8
Average[a]											
Non-S.E.						33.0	13.3	46.3	+13.2 — 9.1	22.3
S.E.				+0.8	+0.3	33.5	12.8	46.3	+14.4 — 6.7	21.1

[a] Each column averaged separately.
Source: See Appendix A.

TABLE B-6
TURNING POINTS, DURATIONS, AND AMPLITUDES OF CYCLES IN EMPLOYMENT IN SERVICES, SOUTHEAST AND NON-SOUTHEAST

	Turning points			S.E. lead (−) or lag (+) (months)		Durations (months)			Amplitudes		
	Init. Trough	Peak	Term. Trough	Peak	Trough	Expan.	Contr.	Full Cycle	Expan.	Contr.	Full Cycle
Cycle I											
Non-S.E.	9/45	12/48	11/49	−1.0	0.0	39.0	11.0	50.0	+13.8	−0.9	14.7
S.E.	10/45	11/48	11/49			37.0	12.0	49.0	+14.0	−0.6	14.6
Cycle II											
Non-S.E.	11/49	10/53	3/54	0.0	0.0	47.0	5.0	52.0	+9.9	−0.3	10.2
S.E.	11/49	10/53	3/54			47.0	5.0	52.0	+17.2	−0.1	17.3
Cycle III											
Non-S.E.	3/54	8/57	4/58	+1.0	+2.0	41.0	8.0	49.0	+8.8	−1.3	10.1
S.E.	3/54	9/57	6/58			42.0	9.0	51.0	+12.1	−0.2	12.3
Cycle IV											
Non-S.E.	4/58	4/60	4/61	+7.0	−2.0	24.0	12.0	36.0	+6.1	+0.4	5.7
S.E.	6/58	11/60	2/61			29.0	3.0	32.0	+7.5	−0.1	7.6
Average[a]											
Non-S.E.				+1.8	0.0	37.8	9.0	46.8	+9.7	−0.5	10.2
S.E.						38.8	7.3	46.0	+12.7	−0.3	13.0

[a] Each column averaged separately.
Source: See Appendix A.

TABLE B-7
TURNING POINTS, DURATIONS, AND AMPLITUDES OF CYCLES IN MINING EMPLOYMENT, SOUTHEAST AND NON-SOUTHEAST

Cycle	Turning points			S.E. lead (−) or lag (+) (months)		Durations (months)			Amplitudes		
	Init. Trough	Peak	Term. Trough	Peak	Trough	Expan.	Contr.	Full Cycle	Expan.	Contr.	Full Cycle
Cycle I											
Non-S.E.	10/45	12/48	10/49	−3.0	0.0	38.0	10.0	48.0	+20.0	−18.3	38.3
S.E.	10/45	9/48	10/49			35.0	13.0	48.0	+19.0	−27.6	46.6
Cycle II											
Non-S.E.	10/49	1/53	9/54	+6.0	0.0	39.0	20.0	59.0	+ 9.6	−11.4	21.0
S.E.	10/49	7/53	9/54			45.0	14.0	59.0	+ 0.3	−13.7	14.0
Cycle III											
Non-S.E.	9/54	7/57	8/58	0.0	−1.0	34.0	13.0	47.0	+ 5.8	−11.5	17.3
S.E.	9/54	7/57	7/58			34.0	12.0	46.0	+15.8	−14.5	30.3
Cycle IV											
Non-S.E.	8/58	4/60	4/61	0.0	−3.0	20.0	12.0	32.0	— 1.8	— 8.0	6.2
S.E.	7/58	4/60	1/61			21.0	9.0	30.0	— 5.8	— 6.3	0.5
Average[a]											
Non-S.E.				+0.8	−1.0	32.8	13.8	46.5	+ 8.4	−12.3	20.7
S.E.						33.8	12.0	45.8	+ 7.3	−15.1	22.9

[a] Each column averaged separately.
Source: See Appendix A.

TABLE B-8
TURNING POINTS, DURATIONS, AND AMPLITUDES OF CYCLES IN CONTRACT CONSTRUCTION EMPLOYMENT, SOUTHEAST AND NON-SOUTHEAST

	Turning points				S.E. lead (—) or lag (+) (months)		Durations (months)			Amplitudes		
	Init. Trough	Peak	Term. Trough		Peak	Trough	Expan.	Contr.	Full Cycle	Expan.	Contr.	Full Cycle
Cycle I												
Non-S.E.	5/45	12/48	2/50		—6.0	—8.0	43.0	14.0	57.0	+63.0 — 6.2		69.2
S.E.	10/45	6/48	6/49				32.0	12.0	44.0	+55.8 — 7.5		63.3
Cycle II												
Non-S.E.	2/50	3/53	7/53		—2.0	+13.0	37.0	4.0	41.0	+16.9 — 2.5		19.4
S.E.	6/49	1/53	8/54				43.0	19.0	62.0	+36.2 —14.1		50.3
Cycle III												
Non-S.E.	7/53	6/56	6/58		+14.0	—4.0	35.0	24.0	59.0	+19.8 —14.2		34.0
S.E.	8/54	10/57	2/58				38.0	4.0	42.0	+16.5 — 3.7		20.2
Cycle IV												
Non-S.E.	6/58	2/60	12/60		+3.0	+4.0	20.0	10.0	30.0	+ 5.5 — 4.2		9.7
S.E.	2/58	5/60	4/61				27.0	11.0	38.0	+ 6.4 — 6.0		12.4
Average[a]												
Non-S.E.					+2.3	+1.2	33.8	13.0	46.8	+26.3 — 6.8		33.1
S.E.							35.0	11.5	46.5	+28.7 — 7.8		36.6

[a] Each column averaged separately.
Source: See Appendix A.

TABLE B-9
TURNING POINTS, DURATIONS, AND AMPLITUDES OF CYCLES IN MANUFACTURING EMPLOYMENT, SOUTHEAST AND NON-SOUTHEAST

Cycle	Turning points			S.E. lead (−) or lag (+) (months)		Durations (months)			Amplitudes		
	Init. Trough	Peak	Term. Trough	Peak	Trough	Expan.	Contr.	Full Cycle	Expan.	Contr.	Full Cycle
Cycle I											
Non-S.E.	9/45	1/48	11/49			28.0	22.0	50.0	+10.7	−11.0	21.7
S.E.	11/45	6/48	7/49	+5.0	−4.0	31.0	13.0	44.0	+15.3	−10.9	26.2
Cycle II											
Non-S.E.	11/49	7/53	8/54			44.0	13.0	57.0	+23.4	−11.0	34.4
S.E.	7/49	7/53	8/54	0.0	0.0	48.0	13.0	61.0	+19.9	− 5.6	25.5
Cycle III											
Non-S.E.	8/54	3/57	5/58			31.0	14.0	45.0	+ 7.2	−11.1	18.3
S.E.	8/54	4/57	5/58	+1.0	0.0	32.0	13.0	45.0	+ 8.6	− 4.5	13.1
Cycle IV											
Non-S.E.	5/58	2/60	2/61			21.0	12.0	33.0	+ 8.1	− 6.8	14.9
S.E.	5/58	4/60	2/61	+2.0	0.0	23.0	10.0	33.0	+ 9.2	− 3.2	12.4
Average[a]											
Non-S.E.						31.0	15.3	46.3	+12.4	−10.0	22.3
S.E.				+2.0	−1.0	33.5	12.3	45.8	+13.3	− 6.1	19.3

[a] Each column averaged separately.
Source: See Appendix A.

TABLE B-10
TURNING POINTS, DURATIONS, AND AMPLITUDES OF CYCLES IN TRANSPORTATION AND PUBLIC UTILITIES EMPLOYMENT, SOUTHEAST AND NON-SOUTHEAST

Cycle	Turning points			S.E. lead (—) or lag (+) (months)		Durations (months)			Amplitudes		
	Init. Trough	Peak	Term. Trough	Peak	Trough	Expan.	Contr.	Full Cycle	Expan.	Contr.	Full Cycle
Cycle I											
Non-S.E.	8/45	7/48	10/49			35.0	15.0	50.0	+ 7.1	—7.3	14.4
S.E.	9/45	9/48	10/49	+2.0	0.0	35.0	13.0	48.0	+10.0	—9.3	19.3
Cycle II											
Non-S.E.	10/49	7/53	11/54			45.0	16.0	61.0	+ 9.6	—6.5	16.1
S.E.	10/49	9/53	9/54	+2.0	—2.0	47.0	12.0	59.0	+11.9	—5.1	17.0
Cycle III											
Non-S.E.	11/54	4/57	9/58			29.0	17.0	46.0	+ 5.0	—8.6	13.6
S.E.	9/54	8/57	7/58	+4.0	—2.0	35.0	11.0	46.0	+ 7.8	—6.0	13.8
Cycle IV											
Non-S.E.	9/58	4/60	4/61			19.0	12.0	31.0	+ 2.3	—3.5	5.8
S.E.	7/58	5/60	5/61	+1.0	+1.0	22.0	12.0	34.0	+ 2.4	—3.6	6.0
Average[a]											
Non-S.E.						32.0	15.0	47.0	+ 6.0	—6.5	12.5
S.E.				+2.3	—0.8	34.8	12.0	46.8	+ 8.0	—6.0	14.0

[a] Each column averaged separately.
Source: See Appendix A.

TABLE B-11
TURNING POINTS, DURATIONS, AND AMPLITUDES OF CYCLES IN TRADE EMPLOYMENT, SOUTHEAST AND NON-SOUTHEAST

Cycle	Turning points			S.E. lead (−) or lag (+) (months)		Durations (months)			Amplitudes		
	Init. Trough	Peak	Term. Trough	Peak	Trough	Expan.	Contr.	Full Cycle	Expan.	Contr.	Full Cycle
Cycle I											
Non-S.E.	4/45	11/48	7/49			43.0	8.0	51.0	+24.0	−1.5	25.5
S.E.	4/45	10/48	3/49	−1.0	−4.0	42.0	5.0	47.0	+30.2	−0.7	30.9
Cycle II											
Non-S.E.	7/49	10/53	6/54			51.0	8.0	59.0	+ 9.7	−0.5	10.2
S.E.	3/49	9/53	6/54	−1.0	0.0	54.0	9.0	63.0	+15.4	−1.2	16.6
Cycle III											
Non-S.E.	6/54	4/57	4/58			34.0	12.0	46.0	+ 5.7	−2.1	7.8
S.E.	6/54	4/57	4/58	0.0	0.0	34.0	12.0	46.0	+10.2	−1.8	12.0
Cycle IV											
Non-S.E.	4/58	4/60	4/61			24.0	12.0	36.0	+ 6.4	−1.1	7.5
S.E.	4/58	4/60	4/61	0.0	0.0	24.0	12.0	36.0	+ 6.5	−0.4	6.9
Average[a]											
Non-S.E.						38.0	10.0	48.0	+11.5	−1.3	12.8
S.E.				−0.5	−1.0	38.5	9.5	48.0	+15.6	−1.0	16.6

[a] Each column averaged separately.
Source: See Appendix A.

TABLE B-12
TURNING POINTS, DURATIONS, AND AMPLITUDES OF CYCLES IN FINANCE EMPLOYMENT, SOUTHEAST AND NON-SOUTHEAST

Cycle	Turning points			S.E. lead (−) or lag (+) (months)		Durations (months)			Amplitudes		
	Init. Trough	Peak	Term. Trough	Peak	Trough	Expan.	Contr.	Full Cycle	Expan.	Contr.	Full Cycle
Cycle I											
Non-S.E.	4/45	7/48	7/49			39.0	12.0	51.0	+20.2	+0.8	19.4
S.E.	5/45	11/48	5/49	+4.0	−2.0	42.0	6.0	48.0	+31.6	−1.7	33.3
Cycle II											
Non-S.E.	7/49	5/54	8/54			58.0	3.0	61.0	+15.5	+0.8	14.7
S.E.	5/49	12/53	4/54	−5.0	−4.0	55.0	4.0	59.0	+38.7	+1.3	37.4
Cycle III											
Non-S.E.	8/54	1/58	7/58			41.0	6.0	47.0	+9.8	−0.2	10.0
S.E.	4/54	12/57	4/58	−1.0	−3.0	44.0	4.0	48.0	+21.5	+0.6	20.9
Cycle IV											
Non-S.E.	7/58	11/60	3/61			29.0	4.0	33.0	+6.4	+0.6	5.8
S.E.	4/58	10/60	2/61	−1.0	−1.0	30.0	4.0	34.0	+12.9	+0.8	12.1
Average[a]											
Non-S.E.						41.8	6.3	48.0	+13.0	+0.5	12.5
S.E.				−0.8	−2.5	42.8	4.5	47.3	+26.2	+0.3	25.9

[a] Each column averaged separately.
Source: See Appendix A.

TABLE B-13
TURNING POINTS, DURATIONS, AND AMPLITUDES OF CYCLES IN SERVICES AND MISCELLANEOUS EMPLOYMENT, SOUTHEAST AND NON-SOUTHEAST

	Turning points			S.E. lead (—) or lag (+) (months)		Durations (months)			Amplitudes		
	Init.	Term.						Full			Full
Cycle	Trough	Peak	Trough	Peak	Trough	Expan.	Contr.	Cycle	Expan.	Contr.	Cycle
Cycle I											
Non-S.E.	5/45	8/48	3/49			39.0	7.0	46.0	+21.7	+0.4	21.3
S.E.	4/45	6/48	2/49	−2.0	−1.0	38.0	8.0	46.0	+22.6	+0.2	22.4
Cycle II											
Non-S.E.	3/49	6/53	1/54			51.0	7.0	58.0	+9.2	+1.1	8.1
S.E.	2/49	6/53	2/54	0.0	+1.0	52.0	8.0	60.0	+22.2	+1.1	21.1
Cycle III											
Non-S.E.	1/54	7/57	4/58			42.0	9.0	51.0	+12.9	−0.1	13.0
S.E.	2/54	7/57	3/58	0.0	−1.0	41.0	8.0	49.0	+14.5	+0.1	14.4
Cycle IV											
Non-S.E.	4/58	11/60	5/61			31.0	6.0	37.0	+8.2	+0.3	7.9
S.E.	3/58	9/60	2/61	−2.0	−3.0	30.0	5.0	35.0	+12.3	+0.3	12.0
Average[a]											
Non-S.E.						40.8	7.3	48.0	+13.0	+0.4	12.6
S.E.				−1.0	−1.0	40.3	7.3	47.5	+17.9	+0.4	17.5

[a] Each column averaged separately.
Source: See Appendix A.

TABLE B-14
TURNING POINTS, DURATIONS, AND AMPLITUDES OF CYCLES IN GOVERNMENT EMPLOYMENT, SOUTHEAST AND NON-SOUTHEAST

Cycle	Turning points			S.E. lead (−) or lag (+) (months)		Durations (months)			Amplitudes		
	Init. Trough	Peak	Term. Trough	Peak	Trough	Expan.	Contr.	Full Cycle	Expan.	Contr.	Full Cycle
Cycle I											
Non-S.E.	8/47	4/49	2/50			20.0	10.0	30.0	+ 7.4	+0.2	7.2
S.E.	9/47	9/49	3/50	+5.0	+1.0	24.0	6.0	30.0	+ 8.8	+0.6	8.2
Cycle II											
Non-S.E.	2/50	12/52	7/53			34.0	7.0	41.0	+11.8	−1.9	13.7
S.E.	3/50	12/52	5/53	0.0	−2.0	33.0	5.0	38.0	+17.6	−1.3	18.9
Cycle III											
Non-S.E.	7/54	7/57	11/57			48.0	4.0	52.0	+14.8	+0.3	14.5
S.E.	5/53	7/57	12/57	0.0	+1.0	50.0	5.0	55.0	+15.9	+1.2	14.7
Cycle IV											
Non-S.E.	11/57	3/60	7/60			28.0	4.0	32.0	+ 9.5	−0.1	9.6
S.E.	12/57	4/60	7/60	+1.0	0.0	28.0	3.0	31.0	+ 7.2	+0.5	6.7
Average[a]											
Non-S.E.						32.5	6.3	38.8	+10.9	−0.4	11.3
S.E.				−1.5	0.0	33.8	4.8	38.5	+12.4	+0.3	12.1

[a] Each column averaged separately.
Source: See Appendix A.

INDEX

Agricultural employment: cyclical behavior of, 29-31, 110, 111, 113, 114, 116, 117, 128; growth of, 29

Amplitudes: contraction defined, 12; expansion defined, 11-12; full-cycle defined, 12; relative to growth, 6. *See also* cyclical behavior of particular series

Average weekly earnings of production workers in manufacturing: cyclical behavior of, 25-27; growth of, 25

Average weekly hours of production workers in manufacturing: cyclical behavior of, 58-61; growth of, 57-58

Borts, George H., 1n, 5n, 6, 95n
Boschaw, Charlotte, 1n
Bry, Gerhard, 1n
Burns, A. F., 3n, 5n, 8n, 11n
Business cycles: defined, 2-3; during postwar period, 2n, 7

Cash receipts from farm marketings: cyclical behavior of, 23-25, 110, 127; growth of, 22

Commodity-producing industries employment, total: cyclical behavior of, 37-40, 111, 112, 117, 130; growth of, 37

Contract construction employment: cyclical behavior of, 44-47, 133; growth of, 43-44

Contraction amplitudes. *See* Amplitudes

Creamer, Daniel, 114n

Cycle amplitudes. *See* Amplitudes

Cycle relatives, method of calculating, 11

Cyclical fluctuations, measures of, 7. *See also* Business cycles; Reference cycles; Specific cycles

Data, sources of, 119-23
Duesenberry, James S., 4
Dunn, Edgar, 95n
Durable-goods manufacturing employment: cyclical behavior of, 51-54; growth of, 51
Durations, 7, 13. *See also* cyclical behavior of particular series

Employment. *See* types of employment

Expansion amplitudes. *See* Amplitudes

Ferguson, Charles E., 114n
Finance employment: cyclical behavior of, 79-83, 137; growth of, 79
Fuchs, Victor H., 95n
Full-cycle amplitudes. *See* Amplitudes

Goodman, S. S., 116n
Government employment: cyclical behavior of, 87-91, 139; growth of, 87
Growth-stability hypothesis, discussed, 4-6, 115-16

Hanna, Frank A., 2n
Hicks, John R., 4

Industrial composition. *See* Industry-mix
Industries: "passive" or "residentiary," 3-4; "primary" or "carrier," 3-4
Industries, employment in. *See* types of employment
Industry-mix: effect on Southeastern commodity-producing employment, 99-101, 112-13; effect on Southeastern manufacturing employment, 103-106, 112-13; effect on Southeastern services employment, 101-103, 112-13; effect on Southeastern total nonagricultural employment, 98-99, 112-13; method of adjusting for, 94-96; relation to cyclical stability, 6

Jerome, Harry, 5n
Kaldor, N., 4
Leads and lags, 10, 12

Manufacturing employment: cyclical behavior of, 48-51, 134; growth of, 47
McGee, L. R., 116n

Mining employment: cyclical behavior of, 40-43, 132; growth of, 40
Miscellaneous services employment: cyclical behavior of, 83-87, 138; growth of, 83
Mitchell, W. C., 3n, 5n, 8n, 11n

Neff, Philip, 2n, 5n
Nonagricultural employment, cyclical behavior of, 32-33, 110, 111, 112, 113, 114, 129; growth of, 31
Nondurable-goods manufacturing employment: cyclical behavior of, 55-57; growth of, 54-55

Per capita personal income, cyclical behavior of, 20-22, 109, 110; growth of, 18-20
Perloff, Harvey S., 95n
Personal income: cyclical behavior of, 17-18, 109, 113, 114, 115, 126; growth of, 16
Proprietors income, 114, 117

Reference cycles, 3, 7
Regional cycles, effect of industry-mix on, 3

Schumpeter, Joseph A., 4
Services employment, total: cyclical behavior of, 67-70, 112, 113, 117, 131; growth of, 67
Shiskin, Julius, 8n, 123
Significant difference, between U.S. and Southeast, defined, 13
Simpson, Paul B., 2n
Smithies, Arthur, 4
South: growth of, 4; slow-growth region, 4. *See also* Southeast
Southeast: defined, 7; slow-growth region, 6
Specific cycles: defined, 3; method of measuring, 8-13
Steiner, R. L., 5n

Timing, 7, 13. *See* cyclical behavior of particular series

Transportation and public utilities employment: cyclical behavior of, 70-74, 135; growth of, 70

United States, as defined for this study, 7

Vining, Rutledge, 2n, 3, 4n

Weifenbach, Annette, 2n

Weights of particular series in U.S. and Southeast, reason for computing, 13

Wholesale and retail trade employment: cyclical behavior of, 75-79, 136; growth of, 74-75

www.ingramcontent.com/pod-product-compliance
Lightning Source LLC
Chambersburg PA
CBHW032051150426
43194CB00006B/486